A+ *Challenge!*
Resource Guide

Wave Technologies International, Inc.
ACSP-CHRG-7101A
Revision 1.3

A+ *Challenge!* Resource Guide
ACSP-CHRG-7101A
Revision 1.3
©1988-1998 Wave Technologies International, Inc.
All rights reserved.

Trademarks:

ISBN: 1-884486-36-3

10 9 8 7 6 5 4 3

RESOURCE GUIDE

Contents

Foreword

The A+ *Challenge!* Resource Guide presents a printed copy of the sample test questions presented on the Challenge! Interactive CD-ROM. It is important that you use the *Challenge! Interactive* product because it most closely replicates the certification testing environment. The *Challenge!* also has many powerful interactive learning features–such as links to content help files, the ability to select questions by topic and access to targeted individualized reports–that cannot be made available in this reference guide.

The A+ *Challenge!* Resource Guide serves the valuable purpose of providing additional review for the certification tests. At times, you will want to review sample items while traveling or when you do not have access to a computer. The A+ *Challenge!* Resource Guide now makes this type of review possible. Both the *Challenge! Interactive* CD-ROM and the A+ *Challenge!* Resource Guide are valuable components of Wave's industry-leading multiple media approach to learning.

This guide is organized around the courses in the Complete A+ Computer Support Professional Career Pack. Each course is divided into topics and test items are then grouped by topic. Over 1000 test items are included in this Guide. The only questions from the *Challenge! Interactive* CD-ROM not included in this Guide are questions that contained a graphic element and/or required an interactive response. It is important to remember that these sample test items are copyrighted material and cannot be duplicated or reproduced.

Thank you for purchasing this Wave product and good luck with your certification tests and future career.

PC Technologies

INTRODUCTION TO MICROCOMPUTERS

For review of this topic, refer to Chapter 1.

Question ID: 98

The binary representation 0100 is the same as:

A. 3
B. 4
C. 6
D. 8
E. None of the above

B is the correct answer

Question ID: 99

An expansion card has DIP switches set to an IRQ that is defined by binary settings. What is the proper binary setting for IRQ 10?

A. 1110
B. 1000
C. 1010
D. 1100
E. None of the above

C is the correct answer

Question ID: 104

A modem transmits data at 9600 bps. How many characters (bytes) can it transmit per second?

A. 1200
B. 2400
C. 5000
D. 19,200
E. None of the above

A is the correct answer

Question ID: 254

One Terabyte (TB) is:

    A. 1024 Gigabytes
    B. 1024 Megabytes
    C. 2048 Gigabytes
    D. 1024 Kilobytes
    E. 1024 Exabytes

A is the correct answer

Question ID: 290

How many characters are in the ASCII (American Standard Code for Information Interchange) character set?

    A. 127
    B. 128
    C. 256
    D. 258
    E. 1024

B is the correct answer

Question ID: 291

What is the decimal value of the binary number 10101010?

    A. 64
    B. 85
    C. 106
    D. 170
    E. 172

D is the correct answer

Question ID: 292

How many characters are in the IBM Extended Character Set?

    A. 127
    B. 128
    C. 255
    D. 256
    E. 1024

D is the correct answer

Question ID: 293

What electrical state does the binary digit 1 represent?

    A. On
    B. Off
    C. Ground
    D. No
    E. None of the bove

A is the correct answer

SAFETY

For review of this topic, refer to Chapter 2.

Question ID: 53

To prevent damage to circuit components you should use a(n)_____when servicing computers.

    A. magnetic screwdriver
    B. non-magnetic screwdriver
    C. antistatic bag
    D. ESD wrist strap
    E. None of the above

D is the correct answer

Question ID: 189

Voltages in a monitor may range as high as_____.

    A. 500 V
    B. 1500 V
    C. 30,000 V
    D. 50,000 V

C is the correct answer

Question ID: 194

On a wall outlet, which slot is considered hot?

    A. The smaller of the two vertical slots.
    B. The larger of the two vertical slots.
    C. Both vertical slots are hot.
    D. The side of the receptacle wired to the white wire.
    E. None of the above

A is the correct answer

Question ID: 196

Which of the following are most susceptible to ESD damage?

A. Printed Circuit Boards
B. Transistor-Transistor Logic (TTL) chips
C. Complimentary Metal Oxide Semiconductor (CMOS) chips
D. Solid State electronic devices
E. None of the above

C is the correct answer

Question ID: 213

On a wall outlet, which slot is neutral?

A. The smaller of the two vertical slots.
B. The larger of the two vertical slots.
C. Both vertical slots are considered neutral.
D. The side of the receptacle wired to the black wire.
E. None of the above

B is the correct answer

Question ID: 214

On a wall outlet, which side is the phase side?

A. The side of the receptacle wired to the white wire.
B. Both the vertical slots are considered phase.
C. The larger of the vertical two slots.
D. The smaller of the two vertical slots.
E. None of the above

D is the correct answer

Question ID: 216

A client is complaining that every time they touch the metal case on their computer they get a nasty shock. Of the following, which is the most likely cause?

A. The primary winding in the power supply has shorted and is redirecting power to the computer's chassis.

B. The secondary winding in the power supply has shorted and is redirecting power to the computer's chassis.

C. The wall outlet may not be properly wired so that a short circuit to chassis cannot be grounded to earth ground.

D. Electromagnetic charges associated with the flyback transformer are being discharged through the chassis.

E. None of the above

C is the correct answer

Question ID: 227

EMI is caused by all of the following except_____.

A. fluorescent lights.

B. mechanical motors.

C. low humidity.

D. magnetic fields.

E. None of the above

C is the correct answer

Question ID: 228

Electromagnetic Interference (EMI) can affect_____and_____ .
(Choose two.)

A. Monitors

B. RAM

C. Printers

D. Network data

E. None of the above

A and D are the correct answers

Question ID: 234

What is the best grounding source?

A. Electrical outlet ground
B. Workbench ground
C. Computer chassis
D. None of the above

A is the correct answer

Question ID: 235

Which of the following environmental conditions is most likely to generate ESD?

A. Thunderstorms
B. Low Humidity
C. Tornadoes
D. High humidity
E. None of the above

B is the correct answer

Question ID: 237

Which component remains charged after the microcomputer loses power?

A. Diode
B. Transistor
C. Resistor
D. Capacitor
E. None of the above

D is the correct answer

Question ID: 240

Which of the following devices has the least risk of damage from ESD?

- A. Pentium processor chip
- B. 486 processor chip
- C. CRT
- D. SIMM chips
- E. None of the above

C is the correct answer

Question ID: 255

While working in the computer lab, an electrical fire starts. Which of the following types of fire extinguisher would you use to put out the fire?

- A. Class A
- B. Class B
- C. Class C
- D. Class D
- E. You should never use a fire extinguisher around electrical components.

C is the correct answer

Question ID: 256

Your department is preparing a schedule for the completion of several IS projects. The first project being discussed involves discharging several CRTs. You are documenting the steps for this procedure. How long should you wait once a CRT is turned off before you can proceed with the discharge?

- A. A Few Days
- B. A Few Hours
- C. A Few Minutes
- D. You do not need to wait at all.

C is the correct answer

Question ID: 257

Select the true statements from those listed below.

A. High current is generally more dangerous than high voltage.
B. It is safe to assume that most electrical devices are not dangerous.
C. Static electricity of less than 2500 volts cannot be detected by human senses.
D. When servicing electrical devices, always work with your left hand.
E. Always wear rubber-soled shoes when working with live voltages.

A, C, and E are the correct answers

Question ID: 258

As a member of a design team for the new computer room at your facility, you are in charge of making sure that ESD and EMI are not going to be a problem. Which of the following will you suggest to the team?

A. Humidity levels must be kept no lower than 30% relative humidity.
B. Humidity levels must be kept no lower than 60% relative humidity.
C. Fans, generators, and air conditioners must be kept away from the computer equipment.
D. Fans should be kept very close to the computer equipment to insure they are kept cool.

B and C are the correct answers

Question ID: 259

As manager of the Hardware Services team, it is your responsibility to create safety guidelines for your technicians. One of your policies is that jewlery must not be worn on the job. Which of the reasons below justifies this policy?

A. Necklaces, rings, and bracelets can short out components.
B. Jewelry causes EMI.
C. Jewelry causes ESD.
D. All of the above
E. None of the above

A is the correct answer

Question ID: 260

You are managing the purchases for your organization's new computer lab. A member of your staff is responsible for setting up an ESD workstation and has handed you a list of parts to be purchased. Which of the following items belong on her list?

    A. EMI Defibrillator
    B. ESD Wrist Strap
    C. Conductive Rubber Mat
    D. Pentium Processor

B and C are the correct answers

Question ID: 261

The vice-president of Marketing calls the help desk. He is experiencing some strange discoloration on the lower right and left portions of his monitor. When you are dispatched to his office, you determine which of the following as the culprit?

    A. His coffee cup is too close to the monitor.
    B. His speakers are too close to the monitor.
    C. His stapler is too close to the monitor.
    D. He is not wearing a ESD wrist strap.
    E. His monitor was not properly discharged.

B is the correct answer

Question ID: 262

You are training your support staff on the elements of static electric charges. As you discuss Faraday Cages, which of the items below would you hold up?

    A. An EMI Wrist Strap
    B. The Frame of a Computer
    C. A Monitor
    D. Anti-static Bag

D is the correct answer

Question ID: 263

Sheila is getting ready to discharge a CRT. Which of the following should she verify is in her set of tools?

A. High voltage Probe
B. Insulated Leather Shoes
C. A Tacheon Emitter
D. A Grounding Strap
E. All of the above

A is the correct answer

Question ID: 295

While all of the following combinations should be considered dangerous, which of these voltage/current combinations is the most likely to cause serious injury or death?

A. 5 volts at 100ma (milliamps)
B. 120 volts at 5a (amps)
C. 12 volts at 200ma (milliamps)
D. 220 volts at 100ma (milliamps)

B is the correct answer

Question ID: 297

What devices commonly cause Electromagnetic Interference?

A. Speakers
B. Generators
C. Hard Drives
D. Fluorescent Lights
E. Modems

A, B, and D are the correct answers

Question ID: 298

You are repairing a computer monitor. You have observed all of the safety precautions by unplugging the monitor, discharging the CRT, and complying with ESD requirements. You accidentally drop a screwdriver on the neck of the CRT and it breaks. What injury are you most likely to sustain?

A. Electrocution
B. Cuts from Flying Glass Shards
C. Electric shock
D. Concussion

B is the correct answer

Question ID: 318

Select the true statements from below.

A. High current is generally more dangerous than high voltage.
B. Always wear shoes with non-conductive rubber soles when working on computer equipment.
C. Capacitors contained within microcomputer power supplies may store lethal levels of electricity, even when disconnected from the wall socket.
D. Always use protective eyewear or safety goggles when working on computer equipment.
E. Do not wear jewelry of any kind when working on computer equipment.

A, B, C, D, and E are the correct answers

Question ID: 320

Static electricity is also known as:

A. Electromagnetic Interference (EMI)
B. Electromotive Force (EMF)
C. Electrolysis Effect (ELE)
D. Electrostatic Discharge (ESD)
E. Electromagnetic Attraction (EMA)

D is the correct answer

Question ID: 321

Which of the following methods will help prevent static electric charges?

    A.   Keep the relative humidity level no lower than 60%.

    B.   Keep the temperature no lower than 50°F.

    C.   Use a 1:20 solution of bleach and water and spray carpets, draperies, and clothes.

    D.   Use a 20:1 solution of water and fabric softener and spray carpets, draperies, and clothes.

    E.   Use a 20:1 solution of water and fabric softener and lightly spray all electronic equipment.

A and D are the correct answers

Question ID: 322

The purpose of a grounding strap is to:

    A.   Keep the electron levels between you and the computer in balance.

    B.   Keep you insulated from electrical charges contained within the computer.

    C.   Keep a component in place within the computer case.

    D.   Prevent damage occurring to the computer during transit.

    E.   Lock down the computer hard drive to prevent theft.

A is the correct answer

Question ID: 323

Which of the following is NOT a step that must be performed when setting up an ESD workstation?

    A.   Put on the wrist strap and connect it to the computer chassis.

    B.   Place a conductive rubber mat on a suitable work surface.

    C.   Connect the second wire on the wrist strap to the computer's power supply.

    D.   Place the computer on a conductive rubber mat.

    E.   Connect the wire from the rubber mat to the computer chassis.

C is the correct answer

Question ID: 324

If you need to discharge a capacitor with a rating of 300 volts, what should be the minimum rated resistance of the power resistor?

    A. 10,000 ohms

    B. 20,000 ohms

    C. 30,000 ohms

    D. 40,000 ohms

    E. 50,000 ohms

C is the correct answer

Question ID: 325

Which of the following electronic components may have specific disposal guidelines?

    A. Batteries

    B. Printer Toner Cartridges

    C. Network Interface Cards

    D. Keyboards

    E. CD-ROMs

A is the correct answer

MICROCOMPUTER COMPONENTS

For review of this topic, refer to Chapter 3.

Question ID: 30

Basic system configuration information is stored in _____.

    A. ROM
    B. RAM
    C. CMOS
    D. DMA
    E. None of the above

C is the correct answer

Question ID: 31

A measurement useful in determining overall computer performance and speed is:

    A. Megahertz
    B. CPU
    C. Memory
    D. Available ROM
    E. None of the above

A is the correct answer

Question ID: 34

The 80286 computer was designed for the_____bus. (Mark all that apply)

    A. IDE
    B. AT
    C. ISA
    D. MCA

B and C are the correct answers

Question ID: 36

Another term for VESA Local Bus is:

A. PCI
B. VL Bus
C. VM Bus
D. VLSI

B is the correct answer

Question ID: 40

PCMCIA cards were initially based on a_____architecture.

A. 8-bit
B. 16-bit
C. 32-bit
D. 64-bit
E. None of the above

B is the correct answer

Question ID: 41

Random Access Memory (RAM) is volatile memory that the computer uses to store lines of code. Which of the following statements is correct?

A. RAM is stored in a computer's power supply.
B. All information in RAM is lost when power is removed from the computer.
C. Data in RAM is permanent and cannot be changed.
D. RAM contains instructions for starting the PC.
E. None of the above

B is the correct answer

Question ID: 42

The difference between a 486SX chip and a 486DX chip is that the DX chip has a built-in functional _____.

    A.   Memory chip
    B.   Booster Chip
    C.   16-bit chip
    D.   Math Coprocessor
    E.   None of the above

D is the correct answer

Question ID: 43

Which of the following statements are true of PCMCIA devices (PC cards)? (Choose all that apply.)

    A.   They have the ability to execute programs without having to download them to conventional memory.
    B.   Socket Services, a software interface, links PC cards to Intel architecture.
    C.   The host immediately gets information from the card regarding its configuration and capabilities.
    D.   The Card Identification Structure (CIS), allows cards to fully describe themselves so other devices can quickly get the information they need.
    E.   All of the above

E is the correct answer

Question ID: 45

If a computer appears to be running too hot, what device can help absorb excess heat generated by the microprocessor?

    A.   Heat Sink
    B.   Buffer
    C.   Enhanced Processor Chip
    D.   Fan Element
    E.   None of the above

A is the correct answer

Question ID: 47

The MCA bus supports both_____architectures.

    A. 8-bit and 16-bit
    B. 16-bit and 32-bit
    C. 16-bit and 24-bit
    D. 8-bit and 24-bit
    E. None of the above

B is the correct answer

Question ID: 48

A SCSI (type I or type II) interface supports up to_____intelligent devices.

    A. two
    B. six
    C. seven
    D. eight

C is the correct answer

Question ID: 49

The RAID Advisory Board defines_____levels of RAID technology.

    A. five
    B. six
    C. eight
    D. nine

D is the correct answer

Question ID: 56

Which chips have multitasking capabilities? (Check all that apply)

A. 8086
B. 8088
C. 80386
D. 80486
E. Pentium

C, D, and E are the correct answers

Question ID: 57

The POST test is performed by which of the following:

A. The boot record.
B. The BASIC ROM chips.
C. The ROM BIOS chip.
D. The Disk Operating System.
E. None of the above

C is the correct answer

Question ID: 59

Which data interface supports the fastest transfer rate?

A. IDE
B. EIDE
C. SCSI
D. Parallel
E. None of the above

C is the correct answer

Question ID: 60

Which devices on a SCSI chain require termination?

    A. All devices
    B. The last device on each end of the chain
    C. Every other device
    D. Only hard drives
    E. None of the above

B is the correct answer

Question ID: 62

The binary address of the SCSI host adapter is_____.

    A. 0101
    B. 0111
    C. 1010
    D. 1000
    E. None of the above

B is the correct answer

Question ID: 67

With respect to hard disk drives the term RAID means:

    A. A virus that spreads itself onto many workstations in a short time through a network.
    B. Redundant Array of Inexpensive Disks.
    C. Redundant Array of Interconnected Disks.
    D. Redundant Array of Independent Disks.
    E. None of the above

B and D are the correct answers

Question ID: 75

Which interface has the fastest access time?

    A. Serial
    B. Floppy Drive
    C. Parallel
    D. SCSI

D is the correct answer

Question ID: 97

Which of the following provides fastest data access?

    A. RAM
    B. Floppy
    C. CD ROM
    D. Hard Drive
    E. None of the above

A is the correct answer

Question ID: 100

Color monitors use_____electron guns.

    A. 3
    B. 8
    C. 16
    D. 4
    E. None of the above

A is the correct answer

Question ID: 107

Which of the following statements are true? (Choose all that apply.)

    A. Bus speed is a measurement of how fast data can be transferred across the bus.

    B. The adapter slot closest to the processor in a MCA system must always contain the video adapter.

    C. Bandwidth is a measurement of how much data can be carried on a bus, a cable, etc.

    D. Bus mastering is a process whereby devices can take control of the system bus.

    E. All of the above

A, C, and D are the correct answers

Question ID: 121

If you had a monitor which displayed 640 x 480 in 16 colors you would have which of the following?

    A. CGA

    B. VGA

    C. EGA

    D. XGA

    E. None of the above

B is the correct answer

Question ID: 132

Which of the following describes a non-interlaced monitor?

    A. The pixels on the screen are illuminated from right to left, bottom to top.

    B. Three electron guns shoot electron beams that are not in sync with one another.

    C. All even rows are illuminated on the screen, then all odd rows are illuminated.

    D. All the rows on the screen are scanned in one pass.

    E. None of the above

D is the correct answer

Question ID: 134

An EGA display in 16 color mode has a resolution of:

    A.   720 x 348
    B.   640 x 480
    C.   640 x 350
    D.   1024 x 768
    E.   None of the above

C is the correct answer

Question ID: 135

A SVGA monitor displaying 16 colors has a resolution of:

    A.   640 x 480
    B.   1024 x 768
    C.   800 x 600
    D.   720 x 348
    E.   None of the above

C is the correct answer

Question ID: 238

What makes a loud grinding noise when the hard drive crashes?

    A.   A read/write head striking the disk platter
    B.   The disk controller board
    C.   Hard drive planar board
    D.   The SCSI interface cables
    E.   None of the above

A is the correct answer

Question ID: 253

Which of the following are considered output devices?

    A. Keyboard
    B. Printer
    C. Scanner
    D. Display
    E. Touch Pad

B and D are the correct answers

Question ID: 264

Which of the following terms refer to the circuit board that houses the chips that make a PC functional?

    A. Motherboard
    B. System Board
    C. Daughter Card
    D. Planar Board
    E. PCI Board

A, B, and D are the correct answers

Question ID: 265

Which of the following has the widest data path?

    A. Motorola 68000
    B. Intel 80386
    C. Intel 80486
    D. Intel Pentium
    E. All of these processors have the same 32-bit data path.

D is the correct answer

Question ID: 266

You are discussing access speeds with your associates. Which of the following components will you say has the fastest access speed?

A.   A Modem
B.   A Processor
C.   RAM
D.   A Hard Drive

C is the correct answer

Question ID: 288

Which of the following statements regarding computers are true?

A.   Intel processors can be used in Macintosh systems.
B.   200-250 watt power supplies are strong enough for the typical desktop system.
C.   Computer clock speeds are measured in megahertz.
D.   A faster processor will make every component of the computer run faster.
E.   Parallel ports transmit data faster than serial ports.

B, C, and E are the correct answers

Question ID: 326

In a power supply, there are four distinct voltages present. They are:

A.   +120 V, -120 V, +220 V, -220 V
B.   +12 V, -12 V, +5 V, -5 V
C.   +12 V, -12 V, +3 V, -3 V
D.   +12 V, -12 V, +120 V, -120 V
E.   +120 V, -120 V, +5 V, -5 V

B is the correct answer

Question ID: 327

Which of the following statements regarding system boards are true?

A. The system board is also known as the daughter board.
B. One component you may find integrated on the system board is the power supply.
C. Every type of system on the market today uses the exact same system board.
D. One component you may find on the system board is a math coprocessor.
E. Regardless of the type of system board, it will support up to 1 GB of RAM.

D is the correct answer

Question ID: 328

Which microprocessor was the first to support multitasking?

A. Intel 80286
B. Intel 80386
C. Motorola 68040
D. Intel 80486
E. Intel Pentium

B is the correct answer

Question ID: 329

What is the difference between an Intel 486SX and an Intel 486DX microprocessor?

A. The DX has the math coprocessor enabled, the SX does not.
B. The SX can perform faster computations than the DX.
C. The SX was used for Macintosh computers, the DX was used in IBM-compatibles.
D. The DX can emulate a 80386 processor, the SX cannot.
E. The SX can emulate a 8088 processor, the DX cannot.

A is the correct answer

Question ID: 330

Each of the following processors use PGA (Pin Grid Array) packaging except:

A. AMD K6
B. Cyrix 6x86MX
C. Intel Pentium
D. Intel Pentium Pro
E. Intel Pentium II

E is the correct answer

Question ID: 331

Which of the following statements is true in regards to MMX technology?

A. There are 57 new instructions on the microprocessor designed to increase performance of video, audio, and graphics.
B. MMX technology can only be found on Intel-manufactured microprocessors.
C. A process called Single Instruction Multiple Data allows one instruction to perform the same function on multiple pieces of data.
D. More cache is present on MMX microprocessors that allows more instructions and data to be stored on the chip.
E. Pentium II microprocessors do not utilize MMX technology.

A, C, and D are the correct answers

Question ID: 333

Most IBM PS/2 system utilize a(n)_____bus structure.

A. ISA
B. EISA
C. MCA
D. PCI
E. SCSI

C is the correct answer

Question ID: 335

You have a customer who has a computer with a USB port. They ask you if you can help them choose a Windows operating system that provides full support of USB devices. Which operating system should you recommend?

    A. Windows 95 (v4.00.950)
    B. Windows for Workgroups v3.1 or higher
    C. Windows NT Workstation v4.0
    D. DOS
    E. None of the above

E is the correct answer

Question ID: 368

What is the most widely used type of PCMCIA card?

    A. Type I
    B. Type II
    C. Type III
    D. Type IV

B is the correct answer

Question ID: 373

What is the operating voltage of a Pentium 60 CPU?

    A. 2.7 V
    B. 2.9 V
    C. 3.3 V
    D. 5.0 V

D is the correct answer

Question ID: 374

What is the operating voltage of a Pentium Pro?

A. 2.7 V
B. 2.9 V
C. 3.3 V
D. 5.0 V

B is the correct answer

MISCELLANEOUS HARDWARE

For review of this topic, refer to Chapter 4.

Question ID: 79

Parallel cables best fit which of the following descriptions?

    A. Eight wires are required to transmit data bits.

    B. Eight wires transmit data bits with start and stop bits.

    C. Two wires are required to transmit data bits.

    D. Two wires transmit data bits with start and stop bits.

    E. None of the above

A is the correct answer

Question ID: 80

Data is transmitted from the parallel port in which of the following manners?

    A. One byte is transmitted sequentially on two wires.

    B. One byte is transmitted simultaneously as eight bits, one bit is sent on each wire.

    C. Each bit is sent sequentially on a wire and eight bytes are sent at the same time.

    D. Four wires are used to send 4 bits, one on each wire, the remaining 4 wires are used for parity checking and error control.

    E. None of the above

B is the correct answer

Question ID: 82

You are looking at a cable that has a male DB-9 connector on one end and a female DB-9 connector on the other end. Of the following cables, which one is it most likely to be?

    A. Serial

    B. Parallel

    C. SCSI

    D. Keyboard

    E. None of the above

A is the correct answer

Question ID: 83

You are examining a cable with DB-25 connectors at each end. Pin 2 is crossed with pin 3, and pins 4 and 5 also seem to be cross connected. What is the most likely explanation?

A. The cable is defective.
B. It is a special cable used to connect some unusual device.
C. This is a null modem cable.
D. The cable is an ordinary printer cable.
E. None of the above

C is the correct answer

Question ID: 93

Which LEDs must be lit in order for a modem to send and receive data? (Mark all that apply.)

A. CTS
B. Transmit
C. AL Test
D. Receive
E. None of the above

B and D are the correct answers

Question ID: 101

Which leads are crossed in a null modem cable?

A. RTS and CTS
B. Signal ground and Data Carrier Detect
C. Transmit and Receive
D. Transmit and Clear to Send
E. None of the above

C is the correct answer

Question ID: 112

An optical-mechanical mouse works on which of the following principles?

    A. Mechanically driven plastic disks break beams of light, generating pulses that may be counted.

    B. Location is transmitted to a desktop receiver via an infrared beam.

    C. Infrared light is bounced off a reflective mouse pad.

    D. Location is calculated based on two infrared light sources placed at 90 degrees to each other.

    E. None of the above

A is the correct answer

Question ID: 115

Which of the following interfaces is best suited for receiving input from a scanner?

    A. The serial port

    B. The parallel port

    C. The DMA Access Slot

    D. The SCSI port

D is the correct answer

Question ID: 116

If a scanner does not provide a proprietary interface card to handle data input from the scanner, it should have provisions to connect to which of the following?

    A. Parallel port

    B. SCSI port

    C. Serial port

    D. Multi-Purpose Interface Bus (MPIB)

    E. None of the above

A and B are the correct answers

Question ID: 122

Synchronous transmission is best described by which of the following?

- A. Irregular transmission times without start and stop bits.
- B. Irregular transmission times with start and stop bits.
- C. Regular transmission times without start and stop bits.
- D. Regular transmission times with start and stop bits.
- E. None of the above

C is the correct answer

Question ID: 123

Asynchronous data transmission is characterized by which of the following?

- A. Irregular transmission times without start and stop bits.
- B. Irregular transmission times with start and stop bits.
- C. Regular transmission times without start and stop bits.
- D. Regular transmission times with start and stop bits.
- E. None of the above

B is the correct answer

Question ID: 127

Null modems transmit data in which of the following ways?

- A. Conversion of digital signals into analog signals.
- B. Connecting parallel ports with a straight through cable.
- C. Connecting serial ports with a straight through cable.
- D. Connecting serial ports with a crossed wire cable.
- E. None of the above

D is the correct answer

Question ID: 128

Eight-bit sound cards are capable of producing how many tones?

    A. 256
    B. 1024
    C. 4906
    D. 65536
    E. None of the above

A is the correct answer

Question ID: 129

A single 5-inch diameter CD can store:

    A. 20 MB
    B. 144 MB
    C. 650 MB
    D. 1.2 GB
    E. None of the above

C is the correct answer

Question ID: 142

Parallel ports transmit data_____than serial ports.

    A. Faster
    B. Slower
    C. Over greater distances
    D. Both B and C
    E. None of the above

A is the correct answer

Question ID: 207

The term modem means:

    A. MOdern Data EMulation.

    B. MOdulator/DEModulator.

    C. MOdern Data Emission Module.

    D. Multi-Output Data Emission Device.

    E. None of the above

B is the correct answer

Question ID: 337

A customer calls with a problem. They have recently upgraded a machine from DOS to Windows NT Workstation and need to install a mouse. However, both COM ports are currently in use, while the parallel port is free. What would be the best recommendation that you could give the customer?

    A. Recommend that a switchbox be used to switch between a serial mouse and one other serial device.

    B. Recommend that one serial device must be disconnected for use by the mouse.

    C. Recommend that the customer installs a bus mouse.

    D. Recommend that the customer uninstalls Windows NT and returns to DOS.

    E. Recommend that the customer installs a mouse on the parallel port.

C is the correct answer

Question ID: 338

A customer asks your recommendation on the purchase of a scanner. They will be scanning large high color images and text. From the choices below, select the best recommendation for the scanner interface.

    A. Serial

    B. Parallel

    C. RJ-45

    D. SCSI

    E. Any of the above interfaces would be appropriate.

D is the correct answer

Question ID: 339

On a PC, the_____controls all serial communications.

    A. UART Chip

    B. Microprocessor

    C. Serial Processor

    D. MNP2 Protocol

    E. OCR Software

A is the correct answer

TROUBLESHOOTING AND PREVENTIVE MAINTENANCE

For review of this topic, refer to Chapter 5.

Question ID: 44

The two factors to consider when evaluating a surge suppressor are:

    A. Switching speed and clamping speed.
    B. Clamping speed and clamping voltage.
    C. Switching speed and clamping voltage.
    D. Switching voltage and clamping speed.

B is the correct answer

Question ID: 144

A_____placed between the microcomputer and the wall socket provides overvoltage protection.

    A. battery
    B. surge protector
    C. longer cord
    D. firewall

B is the correct answer

Question ID: 145

The corona wires of a laser printer can be cleaned using a cotton swab and _____.

    A. water
    B. alcohol
    C. laser cleaner
    D. household oil
    E. None of the above

A is the correct answer

Question ID: 148

The print head of a dot matrix printer can be cleaned with a _____.

    A. lint free cloth
    B. thin coat of household oil.
    C. vacuum cleaner attachment.
    D. cotton swab and alcohol.
    E. None of the above

D is the correct answer

Question ID: 150

A monitor screen that does not have an anti-glare surface should be cleaned using _____ .

    A. anti-static cleaner.
    B. soap and water.
    C. eyeglass cleaner.
    D. a lint free cloth sprayed with household glass cleaner.
    E. None of the above

D is the correct answer

Question ID: 151

When cleaning the optical components of a CD ROM, be careful not to knock the components out of alignment because:

    A. reconfiguring can take hours.
    B. the focusing lens can break.
    C. the CD ROM drive will be useless.
    D. you could cut yourself.
    E. None of the above

C is the correct answer

Question ID: 152

Which of the following are anti-virus software programs? (Choose all that apply.)

A. VIR.COM
B. MSAV.EXE
C. AV.EXE
D. MWAV.EXE
E. None of the above

B and D are the correct answers

Question ID: 181

When choosing a location for a PC, which of the following is an important consideration?

A. A wall receptacle must be within six feet.
B. Curtains must be placed on any windows in the room.
C. A place relatively free of smoke and dust.
D. A grounded conductive rubber mat must be installed.

C is the correct answer

Question ID: 183

Integrated circuit chips mounted in sockets can work loose over time. The reason that chips work loose is:

A. Thermal cycling of the chip and board.
B. Natural vibration resonance of the chip.
C. Spring tension in the socket tends to push chips out.
D. Vibration induced by disk drive and fan motors.

A is the correct answer

Question ID: 186

A UPS is designed to protect against which of the following? (Check all that apply.)

    A. Excessive Humidity
    B. Spikes
    C. Earthquakes
    D. Surges
    E. None of the above

B and D are the correct answers

Question ID: 198

Which of the following sources presents a risk factor for virus infection on a PC?

    A. Shareware
    B. Authorized user software
    C. Shrink-wrapped original software
    D. Maintenance personnel
    E. All of the above

E is the correct answer

Question ID: 205

Windows near the location of a PC should have a curtain for what reason?

    A. To prevent sunlight from discoloring the case of the machine.
    B. To prevent UV rays from the sun from destroying phosphors on the screen.
    C. Sunlight hitting the case of the computer can contribute to heat build-up.
    D. Exposing diskettes to radiation levels found in sunlight can cause magnetic holes.
    E. None of the above

C is the correct answer

Question ID: 239

Of the following, which is most likely to be the cause of problems on a floppy diskette?

    A.   Storage of floppies near a magnetic field.

    B.   Generic diskette.

    C.   Reformatting a Macintosh diskette as a DOS diskette.

    D.   Trying to use a 720 KB diskette in a 1.44 MB drive.

    E.   None of the above

A is the correct answer

Question ID: 245

Low humidity poses which of the following hazards to computer components?

    A.   Heat buildup is greater.

    B.   ESD risk is increased.

    C.   Magnetic fields travel farther.

    D.   Electrical motors wear out faster.

    E.   None of the above

B is the correct answer

Question ID: 249

Periodic equipment maintenance is important to minimize the harmful effects caused by build up.

    A.   Oil

    B.   Suction

    C.   Dust

    D.   Both A and C

    E.   None of the above

C is the correct answer

Question ID: 250

A new application will not load. You notice several TSRs running in memory. To make the new application run, your first course of action should be:

    A. Reformat the hard drive.

    B. Update the anti-virus software

    C. Unload the TSRs from memory.

    D. Call the manufacturer of the application.

    E. None of the above

C is the correct answer

Question ID: 268

When troubleshooting a potential problem reported by a PC user, what is the best thing to rule out first?

    A. EMI

    B. Power-related Problems

    C. Software Errors

    D. Hardware Failure

    E. User Errors

E is the correct answer

Question ID: 269

Maxine is drafting a proposal for her superior to procure the proper tools for all technicians in her department. Which of the following should be on her list?

    A. Screwdriver

    B. Internet Access

    C. Diagnostic Utilities

    D. System Documentation

    E. A desktop and a laptop for each technician

A, B, C, and D are the correct answers

Question ID: 271

A user has called the help desk and reported that he has deleted his data from his system. You are dispatched to his location and find that he is running Windows 95. How do you restore the files, keeping the long filenames?

    A.   Use the DOS 'undelete' command.

    B.   Use FDISK to restore the master boot record.

    C.   Run the 'defrag' utility.

    D.   Use the Recycle Bin.

    E.   Use the RECOVER option in the Windows Explorer.

D is the correct answer

Question ID: 300

What documentation should you maintain for each computer system?

    A.   System Inventory

    B.   Service Record

    C.   Past Problem Reports

    D.   Past Problem Resolution Reports

    E.   All of the above

E is the correct answer

Question ID: 301

Which single item, normally accomplished during preventive maintenance, is most likely to stop problems from occurring?

    A.   Cleaning the outside of the cases

    B.   Removing and reseating all connecting cables

    C.   Removing dust from the inside of the devices

    D.   Replacing ribbons and cartridges

    E.   Wiping down the monitor

C is the correct answer

Question ID: 302

Which of the following are considered backup power supplies?

- A. Surge Protectors
- B. Power Strips
- C. Uninterruptible Power Supplies
- D. Power Line Conditioners
- E. Standby Power Supplies

C and E are the correct answers

Question ID: 303

What is the most reliable way to prevent your computer from getting a virus?

- A. Use only software downloaded from the Internet.
- B. Use only commercial software sealed in the box.
- C. Never allow any unchecked software or data on your computer.
- D. Develop an organizational policy against users bringing software into the office from home.
- E. Use a virus detection program.

E is the correct answer

Question ID: 349

A user calls the helpdesk and reports problems printing from his spreadsheet application. Upon your arrival, which of the following would you ask to aid you in the troubleshooting process?

- A. Where is the printer and is it working in other applications?
- B. What application are you using?
- C. Have the proper drivers been loaded?
- D. All of the above

A is the correct answer

Question ID: 356

Which of the following actions should regularly be performed as part of a preventive maintenance program?

    A. Wipe down anti-glare monitors with ordinary household cleaning agents.
    B. Clean the keyboard using compressed air.
    C. Dismantle the hard drive and wipe down the platters with a lint-free cloth.
    D. Vacuum away any paper dust that has settled inside a dot-matrix printer.
    E. Clean the mouse ball and roller with a lint-free cloth and alcohol.

B, D, and E are the correct answers

HARDWARE INSTALLATION AND CONFIGURATION

For review of this topic, refer to Chapter 6.

Question ID: 37

When installing a second IDE hard drive you must:

A. Attach a second cable
B. Load software drivers
C. Reformat the first drive
D. Set the second drive jumper settings to slave
E. None of the above

D is the correct answer

Question ID: 51

The cabling for a IBM-compatible system connects floppy _____ to the connector with the twist.

A. drive A
B. drive B
C. drive C
D. power
E. None of the above

A is the correct answer

Question ID: 52

Before disassembling the computer, run _____ and record all system information.

A. CMOS setup
B. MSAV
C. Defrag
D. MEMMAKER
E. None of the above

A is the correct answer

Question ID: 55

Which DMA channel is used for floppy controllers?

   A. 0
   B. 1
   C. 2
   D. 4 through 7
   E. None of the above

C is the correct answer

Question ID: 74

Which IRQ is generally used for COM1 on a 32-bit machine?

   A. IRQ1
   B. IRQ3
   C. IRQ4
   D. IRQ5
   E. None of the above

C is the correct answer

Question ID: 76

What is the maximum number of IRQs that an MCA board supports?

   A. 8
   B. 12
   C. 16
   D. 32
   E. None of the above

C is the correct answer

Question ID: 77

Which of the following IRQs would not be reassigned? (Mark all that apply.)

A. 0

B. 1

C. 3

D. 5

E. None of the above

A and B are the correct answers

Question ID: 84

Before installing cards into a PC, you should do which of the following?

A. Reconfigure the CONFIG.SYS file to the minimum number of lines.

B. Document the ROM addresses of all currently installed cards.

C. Document the IRQs of all currently installed devices.

D. Create a temporary directory to install device drivers while working out conflicts.

E. None of the above

C is the correct answer

Question ID: 85

Expansion boards are configured in which of the following ways? (Mark all that apply.)

A. The board may have jumpers that need to be set.

B. The board is configured by removing resistor packs.

C. The board may have DIP switches that need to be set.

D. Newer boards may be configured with software.

E. All of the above

A, C, and D are the correct answers

Question ID: 86

When installing an expansion board, what is the best method of determining the required settings?

    A.   Run MSD to map the IRQs after the board is installed.

    B.   Consult the documentation for the board or PC.

    C.   Systematically change the DIP switch settings on the board.

    D.   Remove all the jumpers on the board and reinstall them one by one until the board functions.

    E.   None of the above

B is the correct answer

Question ID: 87

Which of the following statements is true about IRQs?

    A.   Several devices on a PC can share the same interrupt.

    B.   IRQs are stored in the File Allocation Table on the hard drive.

    C.   After processing an IRQ the CPU must find where it left off processing other tasks.

    D.   Each device on a PC must have a unique IRQ number.

    E.   None of the above

D is the correct answer

Question ID: 88

A DMA Channel allows which of the following?

    A.   A peripheral device is given a direct path to the CPU, bypassing the data bus.

    B.   A peripheral device is given a direct path to ROM, bypassing the data bus.

    C.   A peripheral device is given a direct path to RAM, bypassing the CPU.

    D.   A peripheral device is given a direct a path to the hard drive, bypassing the CPU.

    E.   None of the above

C is the correct answer

Question ID: 89

DMA is managed with a controller chip on the system board. How many channels can a single controller chip manage?

A. Two
B. Four
C. Eight
D. Sixteen
E. None of the above

B is the correct answer

Question ID: 90

Which of the following tools is useful for finding a DMA conflict?

A. MEMMAKER
B. Norton's Antivirus
C. MSAV
D. Microsoft Diagnostics (MSD.EXE)
E. None of the above

D is the correct answer

Question ID: 91

What is meant by the term "memory address" in relation to expansion boards?

A. An area above 640K that a device can use exclusively for its operations.
B. An address in RAM that flags the CPU to an expansion board's presence.
C. A unique number assigned to a device and stored in a discrete memory block.
D. Reserved blocks of ROM memory that dictate how expansion cards are integrated.
E. None of the above

A is the correct answer

Question ID: 92

Before disassembling a PC, you should:

A. Place the PC on a padded surface such as carpeting to avoid damaging delicate PC boards.
B. Document all system configuration information including BIOS version.
C. Defragment the disk to make sure the FAT is current so that the disk is readable after assembly.
D. Draw a sketch showing the placement of expansion cards within the PC.
E. None of the above

B is the correct answer

Question ID: 113

What is the maximum number of IRQs in an XT type of configuration?

A. 8
B. 12
C. 16
D. 32

A is the correct answer

Question ID: 117

You have installed a scanner and an expansion card on a 16 bit machine. Which of the following IRQs is most likely to be available?

A. 3
B. 7
C. 10
D. 13
E. None of the above

C is the correct answer

Question ID: 118

You have installed a scanner and an expansion card on an 8 bit machine. Which of the following IRQs is most likely to be available?

    A. 1
    B. 2
    C. 4
    D. 8

B is the correct answer

Question ID: 125

A full-duplex modem allows which of the following?

    A. Transmitting and receiving data simultaneously.
    B. Only transmitting or receiving data at a specific time.
    C. Macintosh computers and DOS-based computers to communicate.
    D. Both fax and data transmissions on the same modem.
    E. None of the above

A is the correct answer

Question ID: 126

A half-duplex modem allows which of the following?

    A. The modem may transmit and receive data simultaneously.
    B. The modem may only transmit or receive data at any given time.
    C. Only computers with the same operating system are allowed to communicate e.g., DOS-to-DOS or Macintosh- to-Macintosh, etc.
    D. The modem must be permanently set in either the data or fax mode.
    E. None of the above

B is the correct answer

Question ID: 272

You are to upgrade a workstation used by the President of your company. Which of the following steps would you perform first?

    A. Unplug the computer.

    B. Disconnect the monitor.

    C. Backup the computer.

    D. Remove the computer's enclosure.

    E. Disconnect the keyboard.

C is the correct answer

Question ID: 273

You are reassembling a workstation after replacing the motherboard. When re-connecting the ribbon cable to the I/O card, what should you look for to line up the pin connection properly?

    A. A small notch in the corner of the I/O card

    B. A twist in the ribbon cable

    C. A stripe on the ribbon cable, designating pin 1

    D. The markings "LPT" and "COM"

    E. A gold pin on the I/O adapter

C is the correct answer

Question ID: 274

You are dispatched to a micro-channel workstation to modify the configuration by adding an internal modem. Which of the following will be mandatory?

    A. PC DOS v5.0 or Above

    B. The Syscon Utilities Diskette

    C. The System Password

    D. The Reference Diskette

    E. The Configuration Utilities Diskette

D is the correct answer

Question ID: 275

You are upgrading a 80386-based system. You have installed 64 MB of RAM, an SVGA video adapter and a 2.1 GB IDE hard drive. You discover that the ROM BIOS does not support these new additions. What are your alternatives?

    A.   Install a newer ROM BIOS.
    B.   Purchase a third-party diagnostic utility, such as Norton Utilities.
    C.   Upgrade the microprocessor to a Pentium class.
    D.   Upgrade the bus structure.
    E.   Remove the new components because they are obviously not supported by this system.

A is the correct answer

Question ID: 276

As part of the departmental upgrade, you are replacing the system IDE drives with SCSI drives. In the CMOS information, you select which of the following for the new drive type?

    A.   Type 1
    B.   Type 47
    C.   SCSI
    D.   User Defined
    E.   No Drive Defined

E is the correct answer

Question ID: 289

Which of the following share the same IRQ?

    A.   COM1 and COM2
    B.   COM3 and COM4
    C.   LPT1 and COM3
    D.   COM1 and COM3
    E.   LPT1 and COM4

D is the correct answer

Question ID: 350

By default, LPT1 uses IRQ:

    A. 1
    B. 2
    C. 5
    D. 6
    E. 7

E is the correct answer

Question ID: 351

The floppy drive controller typically uses which DMA channel?

    A. 4
    B. 3
    C. 2
    D. 1
    E. The floppy drive controller does not use a DMA channel.

C is the correct answer

Question ID: 352

Which of the following statements regarding memory are true?

    A. Most newer systems automatically detect and configure new memory modules.
    B. If you receive a memory parity error it is probably NOT a bad memory module.
    C. System RAM manages the traffic of what is being displayed on your computer screen.
    D. Addressable memory is tested during startup.
    E. All of the above statements are true.

A and D are the correct answers

Question ID: 355

PS/2-style keyboards use a _____ connector.

    A. BNC

    B. AUI

    C. DIN

    D. 9-pin Female

    E. 9-pin Male

C is the correct answer

Question ID: 367

You need to access the CMOS menu settings on a workstation. The user does not have the system documentation and is unsure of which key to press. What is the most common way to access the CMOS menu settings on a computer?

    A. Use the manufacturer's BIOS setup utility.

    B. Press <Control><F2> after the computer starts.

    C. Press <Delete> during the boot sequence.

    D. Press <Control><Alt><S> during the boot sequence.

C is the correct answer

Question ID: 376

Which of the following options are usually configured from within CMOS?

    A. Hard disk drive type and size

    B. Boot sequence

    C. Network frame type

    D. PCI configuration

    E. SCSI hard drive size and tracks

A,B and D are the correct answer

DIAGNOSTICS AND REPAIR

For review of this topic, refer to Chapter 7.

Question ID: 96

What does the modem command ATZ activate?

A. An analog loopback test.
B. Speaker shut off.
C. Reset modem.
D. Retransmit.
E. None of the above

C is the correct answer

Question ID: 138

In which of the following ways can you check the keyboard connector?

A. Put one lead of an ohmmeter in socket 4 and check the remaining sockets for 2.5 to 5 ohm readings.
B. Put one lead of a milliammeter in socket 4 and check for a current of 250 to 500 milliamps.
C. Put one lead of a volt meter in socket 4 and check the remaining sockets for 2.5 to 5 volts.
D. Put one lead of a volt meter in socket 1 and the other in socket 5 and look for 3.5 volts.

C is the correct answer

Question ID: 179

What is the first thing the Power On Self Test does:

A. Initialize the expansion slots, serial, and parallel ports.
B. Reset the CPU and the program counter to F000.
C. Check for the proper operation of the DMA controller.
D. Check for the proper operation of the IRQ controller.

B is the correct answer

Question ID: 190

A POST error message _____ identifies a keyboard or keyboard interface failure.

 A. Keyboard error
 B. 601 Keyboard
 C. General hardware failure
 D. 301 Keyboard error
 E. None of the above

D is the correct answer

Question ID: 191

Standard ohmmeters should not be used to check resistance in computer circuits for which of the following reasons?

 A. ICs are not resistors and have no resistance to check.
 B. ICs do not provide enough voltage to operate an ohmmeter.
 C. Ohmmeters provide their own current, which may damage ICs.
 D. ICs are digital devices, and analog equipment is not compatible.

C is the correct answer

Question ID: 193

To connect a voltmeter to read the voltage of a DC circuit, you should do which of the following? (Choose all that apply.)

 A. Make sure the circuit is closed so voltage can flow.
 B. Connect the meter across the resistance potential.
 C. Connect the meter in parallel with the circuit.
 D. Make sure the circuit is open.
 E. None of the above

C is the correct answer

Question ID: 195

On older disk drives, what may be the cause of intermittent data retrieval problems?

A. The gears that drive the platter will eventually fail.
B. The platters will eventually shatter from the internal stress.
C. Tracks on the magnetic oxide shifting outward.
D. The read/write head is eventually excessively worn.
E. None of the above

C is the correct answer

Question ID: 202

Distortion on the monitor screen can be caused by:

A. A loose VGA cable.
B. "Dirty" data.
C. Electro-magnetic interference.
D. A faulty video card.
E. None of the above

C is the correct answer

Question ID: 206

An Analog Loopback (AL) test does which of the following?

A. Tests the transmitter and receiver of the local modem.
B. Tests the transmitter and receiver of the remote modem.
C. Tests the transmitter and receiver of both modems.
D. Tests the transmitter and receiver of both modems and the phone line.
E. None of the above

A is the correct answer

Question ID: 208

A modem test that checks the transmitter and receiver of a local modem is called a(n) _____ test.

   A.   analog loopback
   B.   local digital loopback
   C.   remote digital loopback
   D.   data parity
   E.   None of the above

A is the correct answer

Question ID: 209

Which of the following tests should be performed to verify that the transmitter and receiver functions of a modem are working properly?

   A.   Analog loopback
   B.   Local digital loopback
   C.   Remote digital loopback
   D.   Data parity
   E.   None of the above

A is the correct answer

Question ID: 210

A Local Digital Loopback (LDL) test does which of the following?

   A.   Tests the transmitter and receiver of the local modem.
   B.   Loops back the received data stream from the remote modem. Test data must be sent, received and analyzed at the remote modem.
   C.   Tests the transmitter and receiver of both modems.
   D.   Tests the transmitter and receiver of both modems and the phone line.
   E.   None of the above

B is the correct answer

Question ID: 212

Which of the following tests should be performed to check the integrity of the local DTE, your modem, the telephone network and the remote modem from the local site?

A. Analog loopback
B. Local digital loopback
C. Remote digital loopback
D. Data parity
E. None of the above

C is the correct answer

Question ID: 220

A _____ error code identifies a disk drive problem.

A. 601
B. 505
C. 6712
D. 2112
E. 10011100

A is the correct answer

Question ID: 221

One long and two short beeps at the end of the POST test indicates which of the following?

A. A malfunctioning monitor
B. A hard drive malfunction
C. An I/O problem
D. A memory malfunction
E. None of the above

A is the correct answer

Question ID: 222

During the Power On Self Test (POST) process, what condition is designated by one long beep and one short beep?

A. All Systems passed
B. Memory failure
C. A hardware malfunction
D. Hard drive failure
E. None of the above

C is the correct answer

Question ID: 230

The Ohms setting on a multimeter can be used to measure the _____ of a fuse.

A. resistance
B. capacitance
C. transient
D. voltage
E. None of the above

A is the correct answer

Question ID: 232

Your modem connection is active, but intermittent "garbage" continues to appear on your screen. What could cause this problem besides a "dirty" line?

A. A loose RS-232 connection
B. Local echo is enabled.
C. EMI crosstalk
D. Each modem is set for a different number of data bits.
E. None of the above

D is the correct answer

Question ID: 233

Which system component should not be tested with a multimeter?

    A. CPU power supply
    B. UPS battery
    C. Printer power supply
    D. Monitor power supply
    E. None of the above

D is the correct answer

Question ID: 241

Pegging the needle on a multimeter is a result of _____.

    A. Too high of a setting.
    B. Too low of a setting.
    C. Improper test type choice.
    D. EMI.
    E. None of the above

B is the correct answer

Question ID: 242

The replacement keyboard locks up in the same manner as the original keyboard. Which component is the least likely cause of the problem?

    A. Keyboard
    B. Planar board
    C. Disk controller board
    D. SIMM chip
    E. None of the above

A is the correct answer

Question ID: 244

What type of POST error is recorded when a defect is found in a SIMM chip?

    A. General Protection error

    B. CMOS mismatch

    C. Parity error

    D. 6 short beeps

    E. None of the above

C is the correct answer

Question ID: 248

Small dots on the monitor screen can indicate problems with which of the following?

    A. The monitor

    B. A video card

    C. A VGA port

    D. Hard drive

    E. None of the above

B is the correct answer

Question ID: 267

You arrive at a workstation that is getting parity errors. You ask the user if anything has changed with their PC recently. The user reports that they installed some memory chips they had brought in from home. Given recent events which of the following can you conclude?

    A. The memory is most likely incompatible with the system.

    B. The memory requires more power than the power supply can generate.

    C. The hard disk has some bad sectors.

    D. The processor is beginning to fail.

    E. There is obviously some kind of EMI problem.

A is the correct answer

Question ID: 270

Socket creep affects socketed chips and is a term used to describe which of the following?

A. Thermal Cycling
B. Clock Cycles
C. PCI Bus Structures
D. Thermal Expansion
E. Bus Mastering

A is the correct answer

Question ID: 277

You are dispatched to a workstation that has a low, grinding sound coming from the back of the PC. You determine that it is one of the bearings in the power supply. What should you do to remedy the situation?

A. Replace the bearing.
B. Lubricate the bearing.
C. Plug the computer into a different outlet.
D. Replace the motherboard.
E. Replace the power supply.

E is the correct answer

Question ID: 278

Karen has called the help desk reporting that her color monitor is displaying garbage on her screen. Which of the following are troubleshooting techniques that you can use to attempt to remedy the situation?

A. Reseat the motherboard.
B. Reseat the video adapter.
C. Examine the monitor cable for broken pins.
D. Swap the monitor with one that is known to be working properly.
E. Replace the power supply.

B, C, and D are the correct answers

Question ID: 279

You are troubleshooting a modem problem and need to try dialing the phone number 555-1212. Which of the following AT commands would you use?

    A. AT E0 5551212
    B. AT D 5551212
    C. AT F1 5551212
    D. AT DL 5551212

B is the correct answer

Question ID: 280

Which of the following items are tested during POST?

    A. The Memory
    B. The Keyboard
    C. The Mouse
    D. The Video Adapter
    E. All of the Above

A, B, and D are the correct answers

Question ID: 287

You are trying to identify a potential memory address conflict. Which of the following displays can use the A0000-BFFFF address range?

    A. VGA
    B. EGA
    C. MDA
    D. SVGA

A, B, and D are the correct answers

Question ID: 348

A multimeter performs the same functions as which of the following?

    A. A VOM Meter
    B. An Ohmmeter
    C. A Voltmeter
    D. All of the above

D is the correct answer

Question ID: 354

The Remote Digital Loopback (RDL) test checks which of the following?

    A. Local Modem
    B. Remote Communications Software
    C. Telephone Line
    D. Remote Modem
    E. Network Interface Cards

A, C, and D are the correct answers

Question ID: 363

Select the SI unit used to measure electrical resistance

    A. Watt
    B. Volt
    C. Ohm
    D. Ampere
    E. Henry

C is the correct answer

Question ID: 369

Emily's cursor movement is very erratic when she is using her mouse. What is the most common cause of this problem?

    A. Improperly adjusted sensitivity
    B. Mouse plugged into the wrong port
    C. Interrupt conflict with a modem
    D. Dirty rollers or ball

D is the correct answer

Question ID: 370

The left button on your mouse is broken. What is the most cost-effective way to restore full functionality?

    A. Send it to the manufacturer for repair.
    B. Clean the ball and rollers.
    C. Buy a new mouse.
    D. Install a new mouse driver.

C is the correct answer

Question ID: 371

What is the most common error associated with tape drives?

    A. Incorrect drivers
    B. Media errors
    C. Incorrect termination
    D. Defective tapes

B is the correct answer

Question ID: 372

What is the recommended cleaning schedule used by most tape drive manufacturers?

A. 5 hours usage
B. 10 hours usage
C. 15 hours usage
D. 20 hours usage
E. 25 hours usage

E is the correct answer

Question ID: 375

Eric has recently installed a sound card and would like to connect a microphone. Where would you tell Eric to plug in the microphone?

A. MIDI
B. Line Out
C. Line In
D. Speakers

C is the correct answer

PRINTERS

For review of this topic, refer to Chapter 8.

Question ID: 153

In a laser printer, toner is moved to the print media with which of the following parts?

    A. Conditioning roller

    B. Fuser roller

    C. Conditioning blade

    D. Transfer roller

    E. None of the above

D is the correct answer

Question ID: 154

Dot matrix impact printers commonly have which of the following pin configurations: (Mark all that apply)

    A. 9

    B. 12

    C. 24

    D. 27

    E. None of the above

A and C are the correct answers

Question ID: 155

In laser printers, toner is transferred from the drum to the print media by:

    A. A strong negative charge on the developing cylinder.

    B. A strong positive charge on the developing cylinder.

    C. A strong positive charge placed on the print media by the corona wire.

    D. Discharging the photosensitive drum by exposing it to light.

    E. None of the above

C is the correct answer

Question ID: 156

The conditioning roller in a laser printer performs which of the following functions? (Mark all that apply)

A. Charges the print media with a negative charge to attract toner.
B. Charges the print media with a positive charge to attract toner.
C. Applies a uniform negative charge to the photosensitive drum.
D. Applies a positive charge to the developer to attract toner.
E. None of the above

C is the correct answer

Question ID: 157

In a laser printer, the fuser assembly performs which of the following functions?

A. Makes the image permanent by cold fusing the image into the print media.
B. Temporarily bonds toner particles to the photosensitive drum to keep them in place.
C. Melts toner particles and presses them into the print media.
D. Adds fuser oil to the toner so that it bonds to the print media.
E. None of the above

C is the correct answer

Question ID: 158

In a laser printer, toner is transferred to the print media by which of the following parts?

A. Corona wire
B. Pressure roller
C. Developer roller
D. Fuser roller
E. None of the above

A is the correct answer

Question ID: 159

How is the printwire fired in a dot-matrix printer?

   A. The printwire is moved toward the ribbon by a lever inside the printhead.

   B. An electromagnet in the printhead is activated drawing the printwire toward the ribbon.

   C. The Sortilege process is employed to activate the printwire.

   D. An electromagnet is activated forcing the printwire away from a permanent magnet in the printhead.

   E. None of the above

D is the correct answer

Question ID: 160

Manufacturers of dot-matrix printers recommend that you use their replacement ribbons for which of the following reasons?

   A. Using a re-inked ribbon may void the warranty.

   B. Re-inked ribbons may not use ink that lubricates the printwires.

   C. The fusible link is destroyed on the ribbon cartridge.

   D. Because printer manufacturers want to sell more ribbons.

   E. None of the above

B is the correct answer

Question ID: 163

A toner cartridge contains which of the following?

   A. Drum, charging roller, pressure roller, and corona wire

   B. Drum, fusing roller, transfer roller, and charging roller

   C. Cleaning blade, conditioning roller, photosensitive drum, developing roller

   D. Drum, fusing roller, developing roller, charging roller, and wiper blade

   E. None of the above

C is the correct answer

Question ID: 164

What are the two options for connecting a printer to a stand-alone computer?

    A. SCSI and GPIB
    B. Parallel and SCSI
    C. Serial and SCSI
    D. Parallel and serial
    E. None of the above

D is the correct answer

Question ID: 165

When connecting a printer to a stand-alone computer using the serial port, what is the maximum length the serial cable may be?

    A. 5 feet
    B. 10 feet
    C. 25 feet
    D. 50 feet
    E. None of the above

D is the correct answer

Question ID: 166

When connecting a printer to a stand-alone computer using the parallel port, what is the maximum length the parallel cable may be?

    A. 5 feet
    B. 10 feet
    C. 25 feet
    D. 50 feet
    E. None of the above

B is the correct answer

Question ID: 167

Which of the following serial printer parameters for the port must be set through either the operating system or the application?

    A. Characters per inch, baud rate, and parity
    B. Printer type, characters per inch and parity
    C. Parity, baud rate, and handshaking
    D. Data mode, parity, baud rate, and handshaking
    E. None of the above

C is the correct answer

Question ID: 168

Which of the following serial printer parameters for the port must be set through either the operating system or the application: (Mark all that apply)

    A. Parity
    B. Baud Rate
    C. Characters Per Inch
    D. Handshaking
    E. All of the above

A, B, and D are the correct answers

Question ID: 169

If Step 1 of the EP process is cleaning, what is the third step?

    A. Conditioning
    B. Writing
    C. Transferring
    D. Developing
    E. None of the above

B is the correct answer

Question ID: 170

In a laser printer, the corona wire:

A. Applies a strong positive charge to the print media to attract toner.
B. Melts the toner so that the fuser roller can press the toner into the paper.
C. Applies a strong negative charge to the print media to attract toner.
D. Discharges static electricity in the paper to prevent paper jams.
E. None of the above

A is the correct answer

Question ID: 171

The photosensitive drum in a laser printer is exposed to laser light for which of the following reasons?

A. The organic coating on the photosensitive drum loses its ability to hold an electrical charge when exposed to light.
B. The organic coating on the photosensitive drum loses its ability to hold an electrical charge when exposed to heat from the laser.
C. Only laser light has sufficient energy to dislodge photons on the photosensitive drum so that toner particles will stick.
D. Laser light heats the photosensitive drum sufficiently to cause toner particles to stick to the heated dots.
E. None of the above

A is the correct answer

Question ID: 172

In correct order, the six steps of the ElectroPhoto (EP) process are:

A. Cleaning, conditioning, developing, imaging, charging, and fusing.
B. Cleaning, conditioning, writing, developing, transferring, and fusing.
C. Conditioning, cleaning, developing, writing, transferring, and fusing.
D. Conditioning, cleaning, writing, developing, charging and fusing.
E. None of the above

B is the correct answer

Question ID: 175

Which of the following is a characteristic of a tractor feed printer?

    A. It can use only one width of paper.

    B. The sprockets are permanently mounted on the platen roller.

    C. The sprockets are adjustable allowing many different sizes of paper to be used.

    D. Tractor feed printers are only used on Macintosh systems.

    E. None of the above

C is the correct answer

Question ID: 177

A disadvantage of thermal printers is:

    A. Heating elements in the printhead fail frequently.

    B. Thermal printers are very sensitive to environmental conditions.

    C. Special heat sensitive paper is required.

    D. Thermal printers are harmful to the environment.

    E. None of the above

C is the correct answer

Question ID: 178

How is ink expelled from the ink cartridge in ink-jet printers? (Mark all that apply)

    A. The ink cartridge is pressurized forcing ink through micro-valves when they open.

    B. A small heating element heats the ink, making steam that forces the ink through a nozzle.

    C. The ink cartridge has a diaphragm that pressurizes the ink. Ink is allowed to flow through piezo-electric nozzles that are activated.

    D. A piezo-electric crystal is subjected to an electrical current causing it to bend and push ink through a nozzle.

    E. None of the above

B and D are the correct answers

Question ID: 281

What command can be used to redirect your printing from the parallel port to the COM port?

A. MODE
B. REDIRECT
C. LTP->COM
D. SUBST
E. MAP

A is the correct answer

Question ID: 283

Select the true statements regarding printers from the options below.

A. The laser within a laser printer can be seen with the naked eye.
B. The corona wires in a laser printer are simply guides for the paper feed and do not require special handling.
C. Each time you replace the cartridge in an ink-jet printer, you also replace the printhead.
D. There are only two connection options available for stand-alone printers: serial and parallel
E. In the EP process, the developed image is transferred to the medium because the medium has a weaker negative charge than the photosensitive drum.

C and D are the correct answers

Question ID: 284

Which of the following are parts of the laser printer fuser assembly?

A. Fuser Roller
B. Toner
C. Page Feed Roller
D. Pressure Roller
E. None of the Above

A and D are the correct answers

Question ID: 285

Select the true statements from the list below.

A. By default, DOS automatically assumes there is a printer on LPT1.
B. The parallel port is tested during POST.
C. Dot-matrix printers cannot connect via the serial port.
D. A laser printer will print faster when connected to the serial port.
E. Ink-jet printers use the EP process to transfer the image to paper.

A and B are the correct answers

Question ID: 304

Printers are generally separated into two categories. Select the two types used to categorize printers from the list below.

A. Impact Printers
B. Laser Printers
C. Ink-jet Printers
D. Non-impact Printers
E. Dot-matrix Printers

A and D are the correct answers

Question ID: 305

Which of the following is NOT part of the six-step EP process?

A. Fusing
B. Developing
C. Writing
D. Printing
E. Conditioning

D is the correct answer

Question ID: 306

Which component in the EP process permanently binds the printed material to the paper?

    A. Conditioning

    B. Writing

    C. Transferring

    D. Fusing

    E. Printing

D is the correct answer

Question ID: 307

The purpose of the transfer roller, or transfer corona, is to:

    A. Remove any residual toner from the drum.

    B. Apply a positive charge to the paper.

    C. Erase the electrical image of the previous page from the drum.

    D. Apply a negative charge to the paper.

    E. Heat the toner.

B is the correct answer

Question ID: 308

What are the two most common interfaces for connecting printers to stand-alone computers?

    A. Serial Port

    B. Infra-Red

    C. Universal Serial Bus (USB)

    D. Parallel Port

    E. Network Interface

A and D are the correct answers

Question ID: 309

What is the default printer port on an IBM compatible computer?

- A. COM1
- B. LPT1
- C. COM2
- D. LPT2
- E. COM3

B is the correct answer

Question ID: 310

What component defines the default printer port?

- A. POST
- B. I/O Card
- C. Computer BIOS
- D. Operating System
- E. Printer BIOS

C is the correct answer

Question ID: 311

Michelle has a new printer that needs to be connected to her serial port. When configuring this printer, what parameters will you need to define?

- A. Baud Rate
- B. Parity
- C. ESC Sequence
- D. Data Bits
- E. Printer BIOS Settings

A, B, and D are the correct answers

Question ID: 341

You are managing the procurement of 10 Dot Matrix printers. The Accounting department will be using these printers to create invoices. You want the highest degree of print density so you purchase which of the following?

    A. 9-Pins and a Heavier Ribbon

    B. 24 Pins and a Standard Ribbon

    C. 18 Pins and a Standard Ribbon

    D. 64 Pins and a Standard Ribbon

B is the correct answer

Question ID: 342

What governs the speed of a dot-matrix printer?

    A. Paper Weight

    B. Printer Memory

    C. Ribbon Quality

    D. Laws of Physics

    E. Printer Processor

D is the correct answer

Question ID: 343

One of the disadvantages of a thermal printer is:

    A. The noise.

    B. The cost of electricity required to operate it.

    C. The lack of qualified technicians available.

    D. The longevity of the paper that must be used.

    E. The cost of the ribbons.

D is the correct answer

Question ID: 345

Most serial printers use standard serial cables for connection to a system. Which is the most common serial connector?

A. RJ 45
B. RJ 11
C. Bi-tronics
D. RS-232
E. AUI

D is the correct answer

Question ID: 346

A factor to consider when using refilled toner cartridges is:

A. The number of times the cartridge has been refilled.
B. The design of the toner materials.
C. The origin of toner materials.
D. The design of the cartridge roller.

A is the correct answer

Question ID: 364

What is the maximum recommended length for a parallel cable?

A. 5 Feet
B. 10 Feet
C. 20 Feet
D. 100 Feet
E. 185 Meters

B is the correct answer

Question ID: 365

What type of cable has a 25-pin D connector at one end and a Centronics® connector at the other?

    A.   Serial Cable

    B.   SCSI Cable

    C.   Drive Cable

    D.   Parallel Cable

    E.   Null Modem Cable

D is the correct answer

PRINTER DIAGNOSTICS AND TROUBLESHOOTING

For review of this topic refer to Chapter 9.

Question ID: 185

Using a paper that has surface roughness greater than that specified by the manufacturer of a laser printer will:

    A. Void the printer's warranty.

    B. Cause the laser to scatter, degrading image quality.

    C. Cause premature failure of paper path components.

    D. Printing to peel off of the paper.

    E. None of the above

C is the correct answer

Question ID: 187

If a customer is using laser printer paper that has a surface finish smoother than that specified by the manufacturer, which type of image defect is most likely to happen as a result?

    A. Broken corners on letters.

    B. A striped appearance on the characters.

    C. Poor toner adhesion, that is, letters popping off or breaking.

    D. Premature wear of paper path components.

C is the correct answer

Question ID: 200

"Finish" refers to which of the following characteristics of paper?

    A. The smoothness or texture of the writing surface of the paper.

    B. The smoothness or texture of the cut edge of the paper.

    C. The composition of the material used to make the paper.

    D. The weight of a finished ream of paper in pounds.

    E. None of the above

A is the correct answer

Question ID: 225

The ribbon of a dot matrix printer should be replaced when:

    A. Letters begin to fade.

    B. The printer suddenly stops printing.

    C. lines are skipped.

    D. The paper constantly jams.

    E. None of the above

A is the correct answer

Question ID: 226

When white lines or unprinted areas appear through the printed output of a dot matrix printer, it is probably time to:

    A. Replace the ribbon.

    B. Replace the print head.

    C. Lubricate the sprockets.

    D. Purchase correct paper type.

    E. None of the above

B is the correct answer

Question ID: 236

A laser printer produces smudged or dirty pages after a service visit. What is the first step for problem resolution?

    A. Clean the toner cartridge.

    B. Reset the printer.

    C. Print several test pages.

    D. Run printer diagnostics.

    E. None of the above

C is the correct answer

Question ID: 282

You arrive on the scene where the Accounting department is having trouble printing. The light is on, showing power to the printer. What would you do to attempt to solve the problem?

    A. Check that the printer is online.

    B. Cycle the power on the printer.

    C. Check all cable connections.

    D. All of the above

    E. None of the above

D is the correct answer

Question ID: 286

You are called to troubleshoot a networked laser printer that is not printing. The self test prints with no errors. Which of the following could be the problem?

    A. The printer is out of paper.

    B. The toner needs to be replaced.

    C. The laser has gone out.

    D. It has been disconnected from the network.

    E. Improper paper is being used.

D is the correct answer

Question ID: 312

You have received a trouble call on a dot-matrix printer that is not advancing the paper as it prints. During your review of past trouble tickets, you find that the stepper motor has already been replaced twice. When you check the printer, you find that some teeth are broken off of the stepper motor gear. What is the most likely cause of this problem?

    A. The gear is physically defective.

    B. The stepper motor has too much torque.

    C. The paper is too heavy for the printer.

    D. The user has been turning the platen knob or pulling paper from the printer while the power is on.

D is the correct answer

Question ID: 313

Your dot-matrix printer is printing a white line on each line of text. What is most likely the cause of this problem?

    A. The ribbon needs replacing.
    B. The print head is to far away from the platen.
    C. The printhead needs cleaning/replacing.
    D. The paper being used does not meet the manufacturer's recommendation.

C is the correct answer

Question ID: 314

John is complaining about a thin vertical line on every page that he prints on his laser printer. What would be the first component that you would change to try to resolve this problem?

    A. Toner Cartridge
    B. Paper
    C. Fuser Roller
    D. Corona Wire
    E. Printer Cable

A is the correct answer

Question ID: 315

You receive a call from a user saying that when they print a document nothing is printed. During the course of questioning the user about the current state of the computer and printer, you find that there are no indicator lamps lit on the printer. What is the problem?

    A. There is a bad printer cable.
    B. The printer is out of paper.
    C. The printer is out of toner.
    D. There is a paper jam.
    E. The printer is unplugged.

E is the correct answer

Question ID: 316

You receive several calls from users complaining that the network printer isn't printing. When you troubleshoot the printer you find that it has power and is on-line waiting for a print job. You also notice that none of the indicator lights on the network interface card are on. What would be the first thing you suspect is wrong?

A. The printer is out of paper.
B. Paper is jammed in the printer.
C. The printer is not communicating on the network.
D. The users do not have proper rights to use the network printer.
E. The printer itself is broken.

C is the correct answer

Question ID: 317

You respond to a call on a laser printer. You ask the user to describe the problem and you find that the printer stopped printing after the toner cartridge was replaced. When the original toner cartridge is placed in the printer, it works fine. What is most likely the cause of this problem?

A. The protective shutter on the toner cartridge is broken.
B. The sealing tape was not removed from the new toner cartridge.
C. The electrical contacts for the toner cartridge are damaged.
D. The printer power supply is not supplying power to the toner cartridge.

B is the correct answer

Question ID: 347

This term refers to the thickness of the paper in thousandths of an inch or mils.

A. Micrometer
B. Calibron
C. Sheffield
D. Caliper
E. Weight

D is the correct answer

LANs, WANs, and the Internet

LOCAL AREA NETWORKS OVERVIEW

For review of this topic, refer to Chapter 1.

Question ID: 12

Select the features associated with PC-based networks.

    A.   Dumb Terminals
    B.   Centralized Storage
    C.   Centralized Administration
    D.   Centralized Processing
    E.   Intelligent Workstations

B, C, and E are the correct answers

Question ID: 13

Select the true statements from the list below.

    A.   Wide area networks link local area networks.
    B.   WANs typically encompass an entire building, while LANs encompass one floor or department.
    C.   Wide area networks provide centralized management; local area networks provide distributed management.
    D.   Wide area networks and local area networks offer similar services.

A and D are the correct answers

Question ID: 14

Disk mirroring and disk duplexing are an example of:

    A.   Centralized Security
    B.   Fault Tolerance
    C.   Wide Area Networking Features
    D.   Distributed Intelligence
    E.   Resource Sharing

B is the correct answer

Question ID: 15

Workstations that act as both a client and server can be found in _____ networks.

    A. Client/Server
    B. Legacy
    C. Mainframe
    D. Peer-to-Peer
    E. Local Area

D is the correct answer

Question ID: 16

Your company has three local area networks: St. Louis, New York, and Los Angeles. What type of network would you create to allow the separate networks to communicate with each other?

    A. Wide Area Network
    B. Client/Server Network
    C. Peer-to-Peer Network
    D. Fault Tolerant Network

A is the correct answer

Question ID: 17

Select the true statement from below.

    A. A CAN is more expensive than a WAN.
    B. WAN connections are typically faster than LAN connections.
    C. WANs are typically contained within the same telephone area code.
    D. A WAN's connectivity costs are usually more expensive than that of a LAN.

D is the correct answer

Question ID: 20

You want to install a peer-to-peer network. Which of the following operating systems provide integrated peer-to-peer networking solutions?

A.   Windows 95
B.   Macintosh System 7
C.   Novell NetWare
D.   MS-DOS v5.0 and above
E.   Windows NT Workstation v4.0

A, B, and E are the correct answers

Question ID: 22

Every server and workstation on your local area network will require:

A.   A physical connection to the network.
B.   A NOS.
C.   A network interface card.
D.   A router.

A and C are the correct answers

Question ID: 77

Your organization has a network comprised of 25 workstations and one file server all located on the same floor. Select the term that best describes this type of network.

A.   Legacy Network
B.   Peer-to-Peer Network
C.   Local Area Network
D.   Ethernet Network
E.   Campus Area Network

C is the correct answer

Question ID: 78

Select the term used to identify a network made up of two or more LANs connected by means of a public carrier.

    A.   Local Area Network

    B.   Token Ring Network

    C.   POTS Network

    D.   Wide Area Network

    E.   Intranet Network

D is the correct answer

Question ID: 87

A LAN allows:

    A.   Resource sharing.

    B.   Common applications.

    C.   Good management policies to be replaced.

    D.   File sharing.

    E.   All processing to take place at the file server.

A, B, and D are the correct answers

Question ID: 89

Select the true statements from those listed below.

    A.   A MAN connects networks that are contiguous.

    B.   A CAN connects networks that are non-contiguous.

    C.   A MAN connects networks that are non-contiguous.

    D.   A MAN connects LANs that are located in different states.

    E.   A CAN connects LANs that are located in different states.

C is the correct answer

Question ID: 90

Which of the following would prompt you to expand your LAN to a WAN?

    A. Your company has acquired another company.

    B. You have built new offices in another state.

    C. You have opened a branch office in another country.

    D. All of the above

D is the correct answer

Question ID: 130

A LAN connects a series of _____ workstations.

    A. Independent

    B. Local

    C. Intelligent

    D. Terminal

    E. Identical

C is the correct answer

Question ID: 131

A client wants to set up a network in his office. There are five machines that need file sharing capability. The client wants to implement a network without having to buy another workstation. What type of network would you suggest?

    A. Peer-to-Peer

    B. Client/Server

    C. X.25

    D. Token Ring

    E. Ethernet

A is the correct answer

Question ID: 141

IPv6 utilizes a ___-bit address.

    A. 8
    B. 64
    C. 128
    D. 256

C is the correct answer

Question ID: 218

Which of the following network models can be defined as a group of computers contained in one building and connected by a direct high-speed connection?

    A. WAN
    B. CAN
    C. LAN
    D. MAN

C is the correct answer

Question ID: 219

Which of the following network models can be defined as a network that encompasses a wide geographic area and supports low- to high-speed links?

    A. LAN
    B. WAN
    C. CAN
    D. MAN

B is the correct answer

Question ID: 220

Which of the following are features of the client/server LAN features?

A. Centralized resources.
B. Centralized security management.
C. Resources managed at the workstation level.
D. End user applications execute at the server.
E. All stations can both provide and access resources.

A, B, and D are the correct answers

Question ID: 225

A client/server LAN must have which of the following devices?

A. Bridges
B. Repeaters
C. Cabling
D. Servers
E. Network adapters

C, D, and E are the correct answers

Question ID: 226

Identify the statements that accurately describe the peer-to-peer model.

A. A small number of workstations are involved.
B. Centralized security is provided.
C. Systems both provide and receive services.
D. Clients access a server.

A and C are the correct answers

Question ID: 227

Seven users need to access each other's machines, but not any other machines on the network. No one else has a need to access these machines. No one person has time to act as administrator. What is the best model to use?

A. Client/server
B. Dedicated server
C. Server-to-server
D. Peer-to-peer

D is the correct answer

Question ID: 228

What is the correct term for a network connecting 20 workstations and one file server all located on the same floor?

A. WAN
B. CAN
C. MAN
D. LAN

D is the correct answer

Question ID: 229

What is the common term for a configuration of two or more LANs connected by means of a public carrier?

A. MAN
B. LAN
C. WAN
D. CAN

C is the correct answer

Question ID: 230

What is the name of the software component that turns a standard PC into a network server?

    A. An application.

    B. A network operating system.

    C. An operating system.

    D. Microsoft Windows v3.1.

B is the correct answer

Question ID: 231

What is the term to describe the cable used for connections between the network nodes (servers and workstations)?

    A. MAU

    B. Cable plant

    C. Drop cable

    D. Network Interface Cable (NIC)

B is the correct answer

Question ID: 232

Which of the following terms describes a network containing 23 workstations and two file servers all located on the same floor?

    A. MAN

    B. CAN

    C. WAN

    D. LAN

D is the correct answer

Question ID: 244

Assume you have a legacy network installed at your organization. Which of the following are characteristics of this type of network?

   A. Centralized Processing
   B. Intelligent Workstations
   C. Custom Applications
   D. Dumb Terminals

A, C, and D are the correct answers

OSI MODEL

For review of this topic, refer to Chapter 2.

Question ID: 23

The OSI model consists of _____ layers.

    A. 4
    B. 6
    C. 7
    D. 5
    E. 2

C is the correct answer

Question ID: 25

Which of the following is NOT a layer found within the OSI model?

    A. Physical
    B. Session
    C. Data Link
    D. Virtual
    E. Presentation

D is the correct answer

Question ID: 26

When selecting the network cabling to use in your network, you are actually working with the _____ layer of the OSI model.

    A. Ethernet
    B. Cabling
    C. Network
    D. Application
    E. Physical

E is the correct answer

Question ID: 27

You have been asked to decide between Ethernet and Token Ring for your company's network implementation. Select the layer of the OSI model where these two specifications operate.

A. Network
B. Data Link
C. Application
D. Presentation
E. Session

B is the correct answer

Question ID: 28

Addressing for information packets travelling across your network is the responsibility of the _____ layer of the OSI model.

A. Network
B. Transport
C. Application
D. Data Link

D is the correct answer

Question ID: 29

Select the OSI layer responsible for accuracy in data transmission.

A. Physical
B. Transport
C. Session
D. Application
E. Data Link

B is the correct answer

Question ID: 30

The layer responsible for managing logical connections is the _____ layer of the OSI model.

    A. Physical
    B. Transport
    C. Network
    D. Data Link
    E. Session

E is the correct answer

Question ID: 31

When a PC communicates with a mainframe, the _____ layer of the OSI model is responsible for terminal emulation.

    A. Presentation
    B. Session
    C. Network
    D. Transport
    E. Data Link

A is the correct answer

Question ID: 32

You are using the File Transfer Protocol (FTP) to transfer a file from one computer to another. FTP functions at which layer of the OSI model?

    A. Session
    B. Physical
    C. Application
    D. Data Link
    E. Transport

C is the correct answer

Question ID: 91

Prior to the development of the OSI model, developing an enterprise solution was:

A. Very easy to do, as all hardware was interoperable.
B. Not easy at all, due to single-vendor, proprietary solutions.
C. Mildly easy due the PSI model.
D. Very easy to do because all of the vendors worked together.

B is the correct answer

Question ID: 92

The Physical Layer of the OSI model designates standards on which of the following

A. Network Operating Systems
B. Copper Wire
C. Processors
D. Network Client Software
E. Fiber Optic Cable

B and E are the correct answers

Question ID: 93

Access Methods are contained in the Data Link layer of the OSI Model. These methods essentially:

A. Tell each node when it is their turn to transmit data.
B. Tell each node when to issue decryption codes.
C. Tell each node when to issue a encryption code.
D. Tell each node when to "speak" to the Presentation Layer.
E. None of the Above

A is the correct answer

Question ID: 95

In your building you manage three networks; Network A, B, & C. Which layer of the OSI model establishes unique networking addresses for managing packets of information between Network A and Network B?

    A. Physical Layer

    B. Network Layer

    C. Application Layer

    D. Session Layer

    E. Transport Layer

B is the correct answer

Question ID: 96

The _____ Layer insures the accuracy of data transmission and archives a copy of the original message in case data retransmission is necessary.

    A. Network

    B. Presentation

    C. Transport

    D. Physical

    E. Application

C is the correct answer

Question ID: 97

The electronic mail package Novell GroupWise can provide X.400 mail services. The X.400 services fit into which of the following layers?

    A. Presentation

    B. Session

    C. Transport

    D. Application

    E. Network

D is the correct answer

Question ID: 116

What organization defined the OSI Model?

    A. IIS
    B. IEEE
    C. ITU
    D. ISO
    E. CERN

D is the correct answer

Question ID: 221

How many layers comprise the OSI reference model?

    A. Four
    B. Five
    C. Six
    D. Seven
    E. Eight

D is the correct answer

Question ID: 222

Which OSI level is responsible for breaking large blocks of data into packets in preparation for transmission?

    A. Physical layer
    B. Data Link layer
    C. Transport layer
    D. Network layer

C is the correct answer

Question ID: 223

Which of the following devices operate at the Physical layer of the OSI reference model?

A. Routers
B. Network adapter cards
C. Repeaters
D. Bridges

B and C are the correct answers

Question ID: 224

Identify the layers of the OSI model which can communicate with the Session layer.

A. Application layer
B. Transport layer
C. Data Link layer
D. Network layer
E. Presentation layer

B and E are the correct answers

Question ID: 241

Select the benefits derived from the creation of the OSI model.

A. It adds support for proprietary, vendor-specific solutions.
B. It establishes a common set of communication protocols.
C. It ensures support for multi-vendor solutions.
D. It created one common protocol that must be used by all vendors.

B and C are the correct answers

NETWORK CONNECTIVITY

For review of this topic, refer to Chapter 3.

Question ID: 33

Which of the following are examples of network topologies?

A. Ring
B. Bus
C. Circle
D. Square
E. Ethernet

A and B are the correct answers

Question ID: 34

A bus topology requires:

A. At least three computers.
B. At least two hubs.
C. Termination at each end of the cable.
D. Fiber optic cable.

C is the correct answer

Question ID: 35

You have been asked to design a network for your organization. As a financial institution, they are most concerned about network down time. Therefore, you must recommend a network topology with a very high level of fault tolerance. Which network topology would you select on this basis alone?

A. Bus
B. Ring
C. Mesh
D. Star

C is the correct answer

Question ID: 36

The amount of data that can simultaneously be transferred across a cable is referred to as the cable's _____.

    A. EMI
    B. Capacity
    C. 10Base Factor
    D. Bandwidth
    E. BNC Number

D is the correct answer

Question ID: 37

You have been asked to troubleshoot a computer that is having intermittent network errors. The computer and its network cable have recently been moved to the warehouse where it is surrounded by heavy machinery. What is a likely cause of these errors?

    A. Dust
    B. MMF
    C. Network Congestion
    D. EMI
    E. Static Discharge

D is the correct answer

Question ID: 38

Ethernet and Token Ring are both examples of:

    A. Cable types.
    B. Layers of the OSI model.
    C. Data Link protocols.
    D. Network operating systems.
    E. bandwidth characteristics.

C is the correct answer

Question ID: 39

CSMA/CD stands for:

  A. Common Sense Multiple Access/Computer Device.
  B. Computer Systems Media Access/Collision Detection.
  C. Carrier Sense Multiple Access/Computer Devices.
  D. Carrier Sense Method of Access/Collision Detect.
  E. Carrier Sense Multiple Access/Collision Detection.

E is the correct answer

Question ID: 40

Collisions are a common part of a(n) _____ network.

  A. Ethernet
  B. Legacy
  C. Client/Server
  D. Token Ring
  E. Peer-to-Peer

A is the correct answer

Question ID: 41

Your company has a Novell NetWare network running Ethernet over 10BaseT cabling. You need to replace a network interface card on one of the workstations. Which of the following network cards would you purchase?

  A. A Token Ring card with an RJ-45 connector
  B. An Ethernet card with a BNC connector
  C. A bus topology card with a BNC connector
  D. An Ethernet card with an RJ-45 connector
  E. An Ethernet card with an AUI connector.

D is the correct answer

Question ID: 42

Your network uses unshielded twisted pair cabling that supports transmission speeds of up to 100 Mbps. The cable to one of the workstations has broken and it is your job to replace it. Select the cabling type you would use in this situation.

    A. Category 3 UTP

    B. 10Base2

    C. Category 5 UTP

    D. 10Base5

    E. None of the above

C is the correct answer

Question ID: 43

Token Ring was created by _____, while Ethernet originated at _____.

    A. Xerox, IBM

    B. Apple, IBM

    C. IBM, Xerox

    D. IBM, Microsoft

    E. Apple, Xerox

C is the correct answer

Question ID: 44

Select the characteristics of a Token Ring network from the list below.

    A. Deterministic

    B. Collision Detction

    C. Token Passing

    D. Multiple Access

A and C are the correct answers

Question ID: 45

MAUs are found in:

    A. Ethernet networks.

    B. Token Ring networks.

    C. Bus topologies.

    D. Peer-to-Peer networks.

B is the correct answer

Question ID: 46

You have been given the job of purchasing network interface cards for your office computers. Select the factors you need to consider prior to making a purchasing decision.

    A. The processor and amount of memory installed in the workstations.

    B. The workstations' internal bus structures.

    C. The type of network cabling installed at your site.

    D. The network operating system installed on the file server.

    E. The data link protocols used on the network.

B, C, and E are the correct answers

Question ID: 47

After installing a network interface card, you must configure it. Select the items below that may be involved in this process.

    A. DMA

    B. IRQ

    C. ROM Address

    D. I/O Address

    E. Fault Tolerance

A, B, C, and D are the correct answers

Question ID: 48

To enjoy the full benefits of a Plug-and-Play network interface card, the workstation must also have:

    A. A Pentium processor.

    B. At least 8 MB of RAM.

    C. A Plug and Play BIOS.

    D. A Plug and Play PCI bus slot.

    E. An operating system that supports Plug and Play technology.

C and E are the correct answers

Question ID: 79

You need to connect a workstation, located in a warehouse, to the company's network. Since there is heavy electrical equipment located close to the workstation, you are very concerned about EMI. Which cable type will provide the most protection against EMI?

    A. Unshielded Twisted Pair

    B. 10Base2 Thin Coax

    C. 10Base5 Thick Coax

    D. Fiber Optic

    E. Shielded Twisted Pair

D is the correct answer

Question ID: 80

MAU stands for:

    A. Multistation Access Unit.

    B. Multiple Adapter Units.

    C. Main Analog Unit.

    D. Manageable Access Unit.

    E. Main Access Unit.

A is the correct answer

Question ID: 98

You are the PC Support Supervisor and have to explain the different types of topologies to your staff. You compare a _____ topology to a string of Christmas tree lights, in that any break will cause the rest of the network to become inoperable.

    A. Ring
    B. Star
    C. Bus
    D. Mesh
    E. Square

C is the correct answer

Question ID: 99

FDDI provides greater fault tolerance than other topologies because:

    A. It has an alternate ring.
    B. It has an Ethernet backbone.
    C. It uses CSMA/CD media access methods.
    D. It uses IBM Type 6 cabling.
    E. All of the above

A is the correct answer

Question ID: 100

Which of the following can provide more architectural flexibility but can require more cable than traditional bus and ring topologies?

    A. Cellular
    B. FDDI
    C. Star
    D. Coax

C is the correct answer

Question ID: 101

Paul has some mission critical systems that must connect to a network at another site. His IS budget provides for a topology that has a very high level of fault tolerance. Which should he choose?

A. Mesh
B. Bus
C. Star
D. Token Ring
E. All of the above provide the same level of fault tolerance.

A is the correct answer

Question ID: 102

While planning the wiring for her network, Teresa makes sure to keep the wiring away from heavy machinery and heating units. This is to avoid which of the following?

A. Bandwidth
B. EMI
C. ATM
D. ESD
E. CSMA/CD

B is the correct answer

Question ID: 103

Which of the following transfers data on the network at speeds of 4 Mbps or 16 Mbps?

A. Ethernet
B. Cellular
C. FDDI
D. Token Ring
E. ATM

D is the correct answer

Question ID: 104

Select the media access method used by FDDI.

- A. Token Rotation
- B. CSMA/CD
- C. Token Attachment
- D. Token Passing
- E. Store and Forward

D is the correct answer

Question ID: 105

You have just installed a new network interface card, however the workstation is not seeing the network. You suspect a hardware conflict. Select the configuration items below that may be causing a conflict with another hardware device installed in the workstation.

- A. IRQ
- B. DMA
- C. I/O Address
- D. All of the above

D is the correct answer

Question ID: 115

Who established the 802.3, 802.4, and 802.5 standards?

- A. CCITT
- B. ISO
- C. IEEE
- D. ITU
- E. ANSI

C is the correct answer

Question ID: 129

In a Token Ring environment, stations can communicate:

A. Anytime they want.
B. When they are in possession of the token.
C. In one direction around the ring.
D. In either direction around the ring.
E. Simultaneously.

B and C are the correct answers

Question ID: 132

Which of the following statements regarding fiber optic cabling is true?

A. It is resistant to EMI interference and generates no radiation of its own.
B. It is resistant to interference and generates low levels of radiation compared to other cables.
C. 10BaseF is the fiber optic specification for Ethernet.
D. Tapping into fiber optic cable changes the signal strength, making it detectable.

A and D are the correct answers

Question ID: 133

Which connector would you use at the end of an Unshielded Twisted Pair (UTP) cable?

A. RJ-11
B. RJ-45
C. RS-232
D. DIX
E. BNC

B is the correct answer

Question ID: 134

A cable that has four pairs of twisted wires wrapped with foil and then placed in a plastic jacket is called _____.

    A. Shielded Twisted Pair.
    B. Unshielded Twisted Pair.
    C. Coaxial.
    D. Fiber Optic.
    E. Telephone Wire.

A is the correct answer

Question ID: 135

A 10Base2 Ethernet network can have a maximum segment length of _____.

    A. 100 Meters.
    B. 185 Meters.
    C. 250 Meters.
    D. 500 Meters.
    E. There is no maximum length.

B is the correct answer

Question ID: 149

Thin Ethernet is also known as _____:

    A. 10BaseFX.
    B. 10Base5.
    C. 10BaseT.
    D. 10Base2.
    E. 10BaseTE.

D is the correct answer

Question ID: 150

A customer calls with a question regarding their Ethernet network infrastructure. They are planning to run a new cable segment to a newly constructed building. The distance that the cable must travel is approximately 315 meters. Which of the following cable types would be most appropriate for this implementation?

A. 10BaseT
B. 10Base2
C. 10Base3
D. 10Base5
E. 10Base45

D is the correct answer

Question ID: 151

Which of the following statements about Token Ring are false?

A. The transfer rate is either 4 Mbps or 16 Mbps.
B. A major factor in Token Ring network performance is the number of collisions.
C. You may see DB-9 connectors on a Token Ring network.
D. You may see RJ-45 connectors on a Token Ring network.
E. The transmission speed of a Token Ring network is similar to the speed of FDDI.

B and E are the correct answers

Question ID: 152

Which of the statements about FDDI are true?

A. FDDI uses a dual counter-rotating ring architecture.
B. FDDI is only slightly more expensive than Token Ring to implement.
C. FDDI can utilize fiber optical or 10BaseT cabling.
D. FDDI exhibits robust fault-tolerance characteristics.
E. FDDI is most often seen as a high-speed LAN backbone.

A, D, and E are the correct answers

Question ID: 164

NAUN and MAU are associated with _____, while CSMA/CD is associated with _____.

    A. FDDI, Token Ring
    B. FDDI, Ethernet
    C. Token Ring, FDDI
    D. Ethernet, Token Ring
    E. Token Ring, Ethernet

E is the correct answer

Question ID: 184

What type of cable has a central copper core surrounded by an insulator, a metal sheath, and an insulating cover?

    A. Telephone
    B. Twisted-pair
    C. Fiber optic
    D. Coaxial
    E. Token ring

D is the correct answer

Question ID: 185

Which of the following access methods is used by Ethernet?

    A. Polling
    B. Token passing
    C. Beaconing
    D. CSMA/CD

D is the correct answer

Question ID: 186

What is the maximum length of a thin Ethernet segment?

A. 500 meters
B. 185 meters
C. 500 feet
D. 185 feet

B is the correct answer

Question ID: 187

What is the minimum distance between a 10BaseT concentrator and a workstation?

A. 100 meters
B. 64 meters
C. 2.5 meters
D. 0.6 meters

D is the correct answer

Question ID: 188

What two connector types are most commonly found on Ethernet adapters?

A. RJ11
B. AUI
C. BNC
D. DB-9

B and C are the correct answers

Question ID: 189

What are the three most commonly used LAN topologies?

    A. Star
    B. Mesh
    C. Ring
    D. Bus
    E. Cellular

A, C, and D are the correct answers

Question ID: 190

What IRQ values are most commonly used when setting up network adapter cards?

    A. IRQ2 and IRQ6
    B. IRQ3 and IRQ5
    C. IRQ3 and IRQ6
    D. IRQ4 and IRQ5

B is the correct answer

Question ID: 191

What is the maximum distance between a Token Ring MAU and a workstation?

    A. 45 meters
    B. 0.6 meters
    C. 500 meters
    D. 185 meters

A is the correct answer

Question ID: 192

Which term is used to describe the lessening or fading of electromagnetic signals over a given distance?

- A. Overhead
- B. Crosstalk
- C. EMI (electromagnetic interference)
- D. Attenuation

D is the correct answer

Question ID: 193

Which term describes the impact that external influences can have on the quality of a signal that is transmitted over metal wiring?

- A. Overhead
- B. Crosstalk
- C. EMI (electromagnetic interference)
- D. Attenuation

C is the correct answer

Question ID: 194

The purpose of beaconing is to:

- A. Determine which station is holding the token.
- B. Locate the boundaries of a ring failure.
- C. Force the election of an active monitor.
- D. Provide time synchronization signals.

B is the correct answer

Question ID: 195

In the 10Base5 standard, what is the maximum network length?

    A. 2 segments < 1800 meters.

    B. 5 segments < 925 meters.

    C. 2 segments < 1000 meters.

    D. 5 segments < 2500 meters.

D is the correct answer

Question ID: 196

A 10BaseT network is normally wired as a _____.

    A. Linear bus

    B. Physical ring

    C. Logical bus

    D. Physical star

D is the correct answer

Question ID: 197

Which Ethernet implementation uses 20 AWG cable terminated at 50 ohms with segments of up to 185 meters?

    A. 10Base2

    B. 10BaseT

    C. 10Base5

    D. None of the above

A is the correct answer

Question ID: 198

What type of connector is used for 10BaseT?

A. AUI
B. BNC
C. DB-9
D. RJ-45

D is the correct answer

Question ID: 199

Which of the following are common sources of conflict when installing a new network adapter?

A. Data path width
B. I/O address
C. IRQ
D. Clock speed

B and C are the correct answers

Question ID: 200

CSMA/CD is the access control method used by _____.

A. Token Ring.
B. Ethernet.
C. Token Bus.
D. None of the above

B is the correct answer

Question ID: 201

Collisions can become a problem on what type of network?

    A. Very small Ethernet networks with little activity.
    B. Large, active Token Ring networks.
    C. Any LAN.
    D. Large, active Ethernet networks.

D is the correct answer

Question ID: 202

Identify the statements that accurately describe 10BaseT Ethernet.

    A. Stations are connected via a 20 AWG coaxial cable.
    B. Stations must be located at least 0.6 meters from a network hub.
    C. Up to 1024 stations are supported per network.
    D. Network adapter connection is sometimes made through the AUI port.
    E. Stations are required to run TCP/IP protocol.

B, C, and D are the correct answers

Question ID: 203

Which of the following is normally wired as a linear bus?

    A. 10Base2 Ethernet
    B. 10BaseT Ethernet
    C. Token Ring
    D. ISDN

A is the correct answer

Question ID: 204

Coaxial cable is normally used for which of the following?

A. Token Ring
B. 10BaseT
C. 10Base2
D. 10Base5

C and D are the correct answers

Question ID: 205

Which cable type is least resistant to RFI?

A. Unshielded twisted-pair.
B. Shielded twisted-pair.
C. Coaxial.
D. Fiber optic.

A is the correct answer

Question ID: 206

A BNC connector is normally used for connecting to _____.

A. Token Ring.
B. Twisted-pair Ethernet.
C. Thick Ethernet.
D. Thin Ethernet.

D is the correct answer

Question ID: 207

Which transmission medium is used by FDDI?

A. Coaxial
B. Fiber optic
C. Shielded twisted-pair
D. Unshielded twisted-pair

B is the correct answer

Question ID: 208

After installing a network adapter card, you notice that the system boots but the mouse doesn't work. What is most likely the cause of this problem?

A. The network cable isn't connected to the network adapter card.
B. The system doesn't have enough memory to support both devices.
C. The network adapter card was installed in the wrong slot.
D. There is an IRQ conflict with the COM port to which the mouse is connected.

D is the correct answer

Question ID: 209

Which type of cable has two conductors sharing the same axis?

A. Twisted-pair
B. Coaxial
C. Fiber optic
D. Shielded twisted-pair

B is the correct answer

Question ID: 210

Which of the following access protocols can be used on twisted-pair cable?

A. Ethernet (10BaseT)
B. Token Ring
C. FDDI
D. Microwave

A and B are the correct answers

Question ID: 211

Which of the following is a disadvantage when using a star topology?

    A. Can be extremely difficult to isolate failures.
    B. If a centralized component fails, the entire network will fail.
    C. A break in the cable can bring down the entire network.
    D. All of the above
    E. None of the above

B is the correct answer

Question ID: 213

Of the following cable types, which is usually considered the least expensive?

    A. Thick Ethernet
    B. Shielded twisted-pair
    C. Thin Ethernet
    D. Fiber optic

C is the correct answer

Question ID: 214

Which of the following cable types offers the most data security?

    A. Thick Ethernet
    B. Shielded twisted-pair
    C. Thin Ethernet
    D. Fiber optic

D is the correct answer

Question ID: 215

Which of the following terms describe the effect of nearby wires carrying signals that interfere with each other?

A. Crosstalk
B. Overhead
C. Attenuation
D. EMI

A is the correct answer

Question ID: 217

Collisions occur when:

A. Two stations try to communicate at the same time.
B. Two stations have the same name.
C. Two stations have the same address.
D. The network is an Ethernet network.
E. The network is a Token Ring network.

A and D are the correct answers

Question ID: 233

Which of the following devices should be installed to eliminate network broadcast storms?

A. Repeater
B. Bridge
C. Router
D. Gateway

C is the correct answer

Question ID: 234

You have a 20 station Ethernet network running on coaxial cable. Two of the stations start experiencing connectivity problems. Which of the following should you check first?

A. Termination
B. Cable break or short
C. Each workstation
D. Server

C is the correct answer

Question ID: 240

The XYZ Corporation is involved in sensitive research. They need to connect several buildings in a campus. They are concerned about security, data integrity, and EMI. They have sufficient budget for any type of cable. What type of cabling would best meet their needs for connecting the buildings?

A. Shielded Twisted-pair
B. Coaxial cable
C. Unshielded Twisted-pair
D. Fiber optic

D is the correct answer

Question ID: 242

Which of the following are disadvantages of using a bus topology?

A. It can be difficult to isolate failures.
B. A break in a cable can bring down the entire network.
C. The cable is expensive and difficult to install.
D. Hubs represent a potential central point of failure.
E. Repeaters are not supported.

A and B are the correct answers

Question ID: 245

Of the six wires in an RJ-14 connector, which are the most commonly used?

    A. 1 & 2

    B. 3 & 6

    C. 3 & 4

    D. 2 & 5

C and D are the correct answers

Question ID: 246

Where would you expect to see an RJ-11 or RJ-14 connector used on a computer?

    A. Keyboard

    B. Modem

    C. Network adapter

    D. Serial connector

B is the correct answer

WIDE AREA NETWORK INFRASTRUCTURE

For review of this topic, refer to Chapter 4.

Question ID: 49

A hub is an example of:

    A. A bridge.
    B. A router.
    C. A repeater.
    D. A NIC.
    E. A gateway.

A and C are the correct answers

Question ID: 50

Dial-up analog services use _____ to convert the digital signal into an analog wave length.

    A. A repeater
    B. A router
    C. A POP
    D. A modem
    E. A brouter

D is the correct answer

Question ID: 51

Select the private line digital service that provides the highest transport speed.

    A. DDS
    B. T3
    C. T1
    D. DS0
    E. 10Base5

B is the correct answer

Question ID: 52

POTS stands for:

    A. Point of Telephone Switch.
    B. Public Official Telephone Service.
    C. Point of Telephone Service.
    D. Primary Office of Transmission Services.
    E. Plain Old Telephone Service.

E is the correct answer

Question ID: 53

Chunks of data being routed through the public network along the best available path is a description of _____ technology.

    A. FDDI
    B. Packet Switching
    C. Public Switched Analog
    D. Ethernet
    E. Data Chunking

B is the correct answer

Question ID: 107

ISDN can provide which of the following?

    A. Caller ID Services
    B. Global Connectivity
    C. SMDS
    D. Speeds similar to that of a T3
    E. Domestic Connectivity

A and E are the correct answers

Question ID: 108

Primary Rate Interface integrates which of the following using a dedicated T1 connection?

A. Voice
B. Video
C. Data
D. Voice Only
E. Data Only

A, B, and C are the correct answers

Question ID: 109

Rick is planning to connect several of his company's LANs to a WAN. He will be using his communications provider to furnish a switched network cloud. His LAN protocol data stream will be translated by a FRAD. What has Rick chosen as his WAN connection?

A. T1
B. ISDN
C. Frame Relay
D. Ethernet
E. ATM

C is the correct answer

Question ID: 137

Sometimes wide-area network services are offered in one geographic region and not another. This is typically due to:

A. Cabling Issues
B. ISP Charges
C. Lack of Demand
D. Various tariffs established by regulating bodies, such as the FCC and PSC.

D is the correct answer

Question ID: 143

Regarding modem-to-modem communications, which of the following statements are true?

    A. Transport speeds are only as fast as the highest speed modem attached to the connection.

    B. Transport speeds are only as fast as the lowest speed modem attached to the connection.

    C. In order for two modems to communicate, they must be the same speed.

    D. Transport speeds are independent.

B is the correct answer

Question ID: 153

Which of the following statements about private line digital services are false?

    A. T1 service provides a transfer rate of 45 Mbps.

    B. T3 service provides a faster transfer rate than T1 service.

    C. T1 service provides twenty-four 64 Kbps channels.

    D. DS0 is a digital service that is a sub-channel of a full T1 service.

    E. Dataphone Digital Service (DDS) is currently the fastest private line digital service available.

A and E are the correct answers

Question ID: 154

Which network interconnection device links dissimilar networks together?

    A. Bridge

    B. Repeater

    C. Router

    D. NIC

    E. MAU

C is the correct answer

Question ID: 166

Which of the following statements describe repeaters?

    A. Analyze the address and data structure.
    B. Amplify the data signal.
    C. Wait for confirmation before sending the next packet.
    D. Operate at the Physical layer of the OSI model.
    E. Improves signal quality and strength.

B and D are the correct answers

Question ID: 167

Which of the following statements describe bridges?

    A. Bridges operate at the Physical layer of the OSI model.
    B. Bridges have access to the physical station address.
    C. Bridges operate at the Data Link layer of the OSI model.
    D. Two types of bridges are transparent and non-transparent.

B and C are the correct answers

Question ID: 168

Learning bridges are also known as what?

    A. Locator bridges
    B. Transparent bridges
    C. Translating bridges
    D. Invisible bridges

B is the correct answer

Question ID: 169

Which of the following statements accurately describe routers?

    A. Due to the overhead incurred by routers, they may not match the throughput of bridges.

    B. Routers allow for segmentation of an extended network into manageable, logical subnets.

    C. Routers operate as remote devices only.

    D. Routers can only support TCP/IP.

    E. When a router receives a packet, it will generally forward it to the appropriate network based on a table maintained in the router.

A, B, and E are the correct answers

Question ID: 170

A gateway typically works across how many layers of the OSI model?

    A. Three

    B. Four

    C. Five

    D. Six

    E. Seven

E is the correct answer

Question ID: 171

What is a brouter?

    A. Another name for a bridge.

    B. A router with bridging capabilities.

    C. A bit-stream router.

    D. A translating router.

    E. None of the above

B is the correct answer

Question ID: 172

Which of the following devices operates at the Network layer of the OSI model?

    A. Network adapter
    B. Repeater
    C. Bridge
    D. Router

D is the correct answer

Question ID: 173

Which of the following devices operates at the Data Link layer of the OSI model?

    A. Network adapter
    B. Repeater
    C. Bridge
    D. Router

C is the correct answer

Question ID: 174

Which of the following devices work with logical network addresses?

    A. Network adapters
    B. Routers
    C. Translating bridges
    D. Brouters

B and D are the correct answers

Question ID: 175

Which of the following network connectivity devices would be used to connect two dissimilar networks?

    A. Repeaters
    B. Bridges
    C. Routers
    D. Brouters
    E. Gateways

E is the correct answer

Question ID: 176

A repeater operates at which layer of the OSI model?

    A. Data Link
    B. Physical
    C. Network
    D. Session

B is the correct answer

Question ID: 177

Which type of device is used to connect incompatible networks?

    A. Router
    B. Repeater
    C. Bridge
    D. Gateway
    E. Brouter

D is the correct answer

Question ID: 178

Which device is used to divide a network into subnets?

- A. Repeater
- B. Router
- C. Bridge
- D. Gateway

B is the correct answer

Question ID: 179

What is the term for a device that combines features of a bridge and router?

- A. Translating Bridge
- B. Conversion Bridge
- C. Rbridge
- D. Brouter

D is the correct answer

Question ID: 180

What is the lowest-level device that can be used to filter network traffic, thereby reducing the communications load?

- A. Brouter
- B. Repeater
- C. Bridge
- D. Gateway

C is the correct answer

Question ID: 181

Which of the following devices should be installed if you simply want to amplify the electronic signal from one network cable segment and pass it on to another?

A. Repeater
B. Bridge
C. Router
D. Brouter
E. Gateway

A is the correct answer

Question ID: 182

Which of the following devices should be installed if you simply want to filter information before passing it on to another network segment?

A. Repeater
B. Bridge
C. Router
D. Brouter
E. Gateway

B is the correct answer

Question ID: 183

Which of the following devices should be installed if you want to break an extended internetwork into manageable, logical subnets?

A. Repeater
B. Bridge
C. Router
D. Brouter
E. Gateway

C is the correct answer

Question ID: 216

Which of the following devices will act as a router for routable protocols and bridges for non-routable protocols?

A. Repeater
B. Bridge
C. Router
D. Brouter
E. Gateway

D is the correct answer

Question ID: 236

Which of the following statements about TCP/IP are true?

A. Was designed for small peer-to-peer networks.
B. Is owned by the United States.
C. Was designed for use on large internetworks.
D. Cannot be used in a UNIX environment.
E. Is not owned by any one person or organization.

C and E are the correct answers

Question ID: 239

Pine company has a small network by number of servers and clients. However, the cabling must cover a relatively long distance. You suspect that there is a problem with degraded signal strength. What is the simplest type of network device that can correct this problem?

A. Router
B. Gateway
C. Brouter
D. Repeater

D is the correct answer

THE INTERNET

For review of this topic, refer to Chapter 5.

Question ID: 55

The Internet is controlled and regulated by:

    A. NATO.
    B. NSF.
    C. IEEE.
    D. ISO.
    E. No single agency or government.

E is the correct answer

Question ID: 56

The Internet is a perfect example of open standards. Select the statement that best describes this term.

    A. Computers can communicate using any protocol they want.
    B. A specific type of computer is not required to communicate on the Internet.
    C. The OSI model does not have to be adhered to on the Internet.
    D. There is no security on the Internet.

B is the correct answer

Question ID: 57

Select the universal communications protocol suite used on the Internet.

    A. Ethernet
    B. FDDI
    C. Packet Switching
    D. TCP/IP
    E. OSI

D is the correct answer

Question ID: 58

199.250.196.1 is an example of:

  A. A digital telephone number.
  B. A communication standard.
  C. An IP address.
  D. A MAC address.
  E. A T1 identifier.

C is the correct answer

Question ID: 59

Select the IP Address Class that allows the largest number of hosts.

  A. Class A
  B. Class B
  C. Class C
  D. Class D

A is the correct answer

Question ID: 60

This service allows you to reference hosts by name, such as www.wavetech.com, instead of using IP addresses when browsing the Internet.

  A. POTS
  B. DNS
  C. FTP
  D. TCP/IP
  E. HTTP

B is the correct answer

Question ID: 61

Which of the following statements are true?

    A. Each host on an IP network must have a unique address.
    B. Intranets differ from the Internet in that they are not open to the general public.
    C. .COM is an example of a domain.
    D. An IP address consists of 3 octets.
    E. The Internet is regulated by the ISO.

A, B, and C are the correct answers

Question ID: 64

You are setting up Internet connectivity for your computer network. Since security is a primary concern, which of the following devices would you include in your design plans?

    A. Firewall
    B. Brouter
    C. Gateway
    D. T-1
    E. DSU/CSU

A is the correct answer

Question ID: 70

Select the protocol that dictates communication and addressing over the Internet.

    A. FTP
    B. HTTP
    C. WWW
    D. MIME
    E. TCP/IP

E is the correct answer

Question ID: 110

During the 1970's ARPANET grew and evolved into a consortium network known as:

- A. ARPANET II.
- B. CERN.
- C. WWW.
- D. NSF.
- E. BITNET.

E is the correct answer

Question ID: 111

In the past, the Internet had to be navigated through which of the following?

- A. SQL calls
- B. API Translators
- C. JAVA
- D. UNIX Commands

D is the correct answer

Question ID: 112

HTML stands for:

- A. Hyper Terminal Message Language.
- B. Hyper Text Markup Language.
- C. Hyper Transform Message Language.
- D. Hyper Transitional Mail Link.

B is the correct answer

Question ID: 113

There is a defacto Internet code of behavior which prescribes appropriate use. When someone on the Internet violates this code by using inappropriate behavior, who enforces the reprimand?

A. IEEE

B. ISOC

C. Internet Control Group (ICG)

D. NATO

E. Internet Users

E is the correct answer

Question ID: 114

Phil is the Senior WAN Administrator for a company that is branching out to the Internet. His company has a variety of hardware systems including: UNIX, Macintosh, DEC-VAX, IBM- compatible PCs, and mainframes. Which computers will be able to connect to the Internet?

A. VAX and UNIX Only

B. IBM Compatible PCs Only

C. Macintosh and IBM Compatible PCs Only

D. Everything Except the Mainframes

E. All of these systems can be configured to connect to the Internet.

E is the correct answer

Question ID: 117

You are the System Administrator for a large pharmaceutical company and you want to provide a secure internal networking solution to your customers (hospitals & clinics). What would provide the access you require?

A. Intranet

B. Internet

C. Extranet

D. WAN

E. Private Net

C is the correct answer

Question ID: 118

Firewall management can be complicated by:

    A. Multiple IP Addresses

    B. Multiple Protocols

    C. Multiple Sessions

    D. Multiple Filters

    E. Users

B and D are the correct answers

Question ID: 119

The IP address of 67.34.4.6 is what class of IP address?

    A. Class A

    B. Class B

    C. Class C

    D. Class D

A is the correct answer

Question ID: 120

Your company wants to have the domain name, ourplace.com. You use your web browser and come across another company using www.ourplace.com. You have to explain to your boss why you cannot use that name for your domain. Which of the following do you cite as your reason?

    A. OURPLACE.COM is a copyright.

    B. OURPLACE.COM is a trademark.

    C. OURPLACE.COM is only allowed for educational domains.

    D. OURPLACE.COM is in use and your domain must be unique.

D is the correct answer

Question ID: 121

What is the name of the organization that registers domains in North America?

A. InterDom
B. InterNIC
C. InterREG
D. InterNAME

B is the correct answer

Question ID: 122

An advantage of using a domain name is:

A. Users do not have to remember an IP address to get to your site.
B. Users do not have to remember the HTML address to get to your site.
C. Domain names are faster than IP addresses.
D. Users do not have to remember UNIX addresses to get to your site.
E. All of the above

A is the correct answer

Question ID: 155

The IP address of 199.250.196.1:

A. Is a Class A IP address.
B. Is a Class B IP address.
C. Is a Class C IP address.
D. Is a Class D IP address.
E. Is a Class E IP address

C is the correct answer

Question ID: 235

You are setting up a large network that will eventually connect to the Internet. Which protocol should you use?

A. NetBEUI
B. DLC
C. IPX/SPX
D. TCP/IP

D is the correct answer

Question ID: 237

What is the protocol used on the Internet?

A. TCP/IP
B. NetBEUI
C. IPX/SPX
D. AppleTalk
E. DLC

A is the correct answer

Question ID: 238

You are planning to connect you small LAN directly to the Internet. Which protocol should you use?

A. NetBEUI
B. IPX/SPX
C. DLC
D. TCP/IP

D is the correct answer

Question ID: 243

Which of the following are considered top-level domains on the Internet?

A. FTP
B. COM
C. GOV
D. MIL
E. ORG

B, C, D, and E are the correct answers

CONNECTING TO THE INTERNET

For review of this topic, refer to Chapter 6.

Question ID: 54

When you click on a word or graphic on the Internet and are taken to a different location, you are using:

    A. Search engines.
    B. Object linking and embedding.
    C. Hyperterminals.
    D. The Data Link layer of the OSI model.
    E. Hyperlinks.

E is the correct answer

Question ID: 65

Your boss wants to be able to browse the Internet from his computer. Select the most inexpensive method for Internet connectivity from the list below.

    A. Dedicated Line
    B. Direct Connection
    C. DSU/CSU
    D. Dial-up Access

D is the correct answer

Question ID: 66

America Online is an example of:

    A. An ISP.
    B. An Internet gateway.
    C. A POTS.
    D. A direct internet connection.
    E. A DDS.

B is the correct answer

Question ID: 67

It is your responsibility to select an internet service provider (ISP) for your organization. Select the criteria you would use to make your decision.

    A. Cost

    B. Support

    C. Available Services

    D. Ethernet or Token Ring

    E. Available Bandwidth

A, B, C, and E are the correct answers

Question ID: 68

Lycos, Hot Bot, and Excite are examples of:

    A. ISPs.

    B. POTS.

    C. extranets.

    D. search engines.

D is the correct answer

Question ID: 69

You have dialed your ISP and appear to be properly connected. However, when you try to browse to a specific Internet site, you are unable to reach it. What would be your first step in troubleshooting this problem?

    A. Delete the Dial-Up Networking configuration and re-create it.

    B. Try using a different login name.

    C. Uninstall your browser software and then re-install it.

    D. Use PING to verify that the host is reachable.

D is the correct answer

Question ID: 85

You have a PPP account through an Internet Service Provider. To configure your Windows 95 workstation to call the ISP and log in, you will need to configure the system through:

    A. Dial-Up Networking.

    B. Network neighborhood.

    C. The System icon.

    D. Windows explorer.

A is the correct answer

Question ID: 86

Select the information you'll need to provide when configuring Windows 95 for dial-up networking to your ISP.

    A. ISP's Telephone Number

    B. IP Address for the Primary DNS Server

    C. IP Address for the Secondary DNS Server

    D. Your Login ID

    E. All of the above

E is the correct answer

Question ID: 123

You are responsible for connecting your company to the Internet. Which of the following are connection options?

    A. Dial-Up Access

    B. Dedicated Lines

    C. Internet Gateways

    D. All of the above

D is the correct answer

Question ID: 125

When searching the Web, the term AND can be used in your search query. By using this Boolean Operator, you will get search results with the following:

    A. Documents that contain the words connected by AND.

    B. Documents that contain AND in the title.

    C. Documents with the word preceding the AND but not after the AND.

    D. All of the above

A is the correct answer

Question ID: 126

You support a network that consists of 50 Windows 95 workstations. When you need to check the IP configuration on a Windows 95 workstation, which utility would you use?

    A. WINUTIL

    B. Network Neighborhood

    C. PING

    D. WINCONFG

    E. WINIPCFG

E is the correct answer

Question ID: 127

To test for the presence of other systems on a TCP/IP network, you would use which of the following Windows 95 utilities?

    A. WINIPCFG

    B. Network Neighborhood

    C. PING

    D. WINPING

    E. PING95

C is the correct answer

Question ID: 128

You would like to follow the route used by your workstation to a remote host. Which of the following Windows 95 utilities would you use?

A. PING
B. WINIPCFG
C. Network Neighborhood
D. ROUTE
E. TRACERT

E is the correct answer

Question ID: 136

Which of the following is more efficient and feature-rich when using a dial-up connection to an ISP?

A. SLIP
B. NETBIOS
C. PPP
D. PPL

C is the correct answer

Question ID: 138

The leased line terminates directly into a _____ that is attached to a dedicated computer which links the local network to the Internet as a direct node.

A. Brouter
B. Bridge
C. Router
D. Repeater
E. Domain

C is the correct answer

Question ID: 139

Direct Connection uses a web server or host directly connected to the Internet. In order for it to be considered a direct connection, there must be no more than _____ router(s) between the local network and the Internet backbone.

    A. One
    B. Two
    C. Three
    D. Seven
    E. The number of routers is irrelevant.

A is the correct answer

Question ID: 146

You manage the MIS division and need to choose an ISP for your mobile users all over the country. What is a key consideration for your traveling users?

    A. Compatability
    B. Access Times
    C. Browser Support
    D. Nationwide Dial-in Access

D is the correct answer

Question ID: 156

Identify the two most popular dial-up protocols used to receive graphical information from the Internet.

    A. PPP
    B. NetBEUI
    C. IPX/SPX
    D. SLIP
    E. XNS

A and D are the correct answers

Question ID: 157

A customer calls with a problem accessing a particular Internet host. Their Windows 95 workstation connects to their Internet Service Provider but cannot access the Internet site www.whitehouse.gov. Which of the following would be appropriate steps to ask the customer to perform to help determine the cause of the problem?

    A. Use PING and see if the desired host responds.

    B. Use HyperTerminal and see if you can access the desired host.

    C. Use WINIPCFG and release all current IP address leases.

    D. Use TRACERT to see if a route can be traced to the desired host.

    E. Use the Dial-Up Networking wizard to reconfigure your dial-up session to the Internet.

A and D are the correct answers

Question ID: 161

You need to configure your Windows 95 workstation to access the Internet. Which of the following steps would you perform to accomplish this?

    A. Install a network client.

    B. Install a network interface card.

    C. Install the TCP/IP protocol stack.

    D. Install the IPX/SPX protocol stack.

    E. Install a modem.

A, C, and E are the correct answers

INTERNET SERVICES

For review of this topic, refer to Chapter 7.

Question ID: 71

Select the protocol that defines how home pages are formatted and displayed within a browser.

A. FTP
B. WWW
C. HTTP
D. MIME
E. TCP/IP

C is the correct answer

Question ID: 72

You frequently send status reports to your boss as an attachment to an electronic mail message. Select the protocol that allows your Word document attachment to travel through the Internet without having its formatting changed.

A. FTP
B. HTTP
C. MIME
D. TCP/IP
E. DNS

C is the correct answer

Question ID: 73

Jbehnke@wavetech.com is an example of:

A. an e-mail address.
B. a domain name.
C. a URL.
D. a host address.

A is the correct answer

Question ID: 74

You are called to troubleshoot a computer that has run out of disk space. Knowing that the computer is frequently used for electronic mail and browsing the Internet, select the steps below that might help you solve this problem.

A. Clear the browser cache.
B. Re-install the browser software, selecting a minimum install configuration.
C. Remove the browser software.
D. Delete any unnecessary messages from the Inbox.
E. Disable Dial-Up Networking.

A and D are the correct answers

Question ID: 75

When using the Anonymous FTP account, the default password is usually your _____.

A. Name
B. Telephone number
C. E-mail address
D. Employee number
E. User ID

C is the correct answer

Question ID: 76

What is the Internet standard login for public access to a remote host?

A. Anonymous
B. Guest
C. Your E-mail Address
D. Telnet
E. None of the above

B is the correct answer

Question ID: 142

You are the network expert on staff. You need a solution that supports file transfers between diverse computing platforms in your company. Which of the following would you choose?

    A. HTTP
    B. MIME
    C. HTML
    D. FTP
    E. TCP/IP

D is the correct answer

Question ID: 144

Internet mail is _____ system.

    A. A Send and Receive
    B. A Forward and Store
    C. A Push and Pull
    D. A Store and Forward
    E. A Cause and Effect

D is the correct answer

Question ID: 158

Which of the following protocols are used on the Internet?

    A. IPX/SPX
    B. FTP
    C. TCP/IP
    D. MIME
    E. NetBEUI

B, C, and D are the correct answers

Question ID: 159

_____ is a utility that is used to maintain automated electronic mailing lists.

A. MIME
B. WINIPCFG
C. LISTSERV
D. FTP
E. TELNET

C is the correct answer

Customer Satisfaction

CUSTOMER SERVICE

For review of this topic, refer to Chapter 1.

Question ID: 12

Why is customer satisfaction with technical service so important?

- A. Customer satisfaction enhances the reputation of your department.
- B. Your own job satisfaction will always improve when your customers' satisfaction does.
- C. Customer loyalty is directly linked to satisfaction with the service provided.
- D. A satisfied customer is the best advertising.

C is the correct answer

Question ID: 13

What are the three skill sets required for successful support?

- A. Technical, Practical, and Interpersonal
- B. Computing, Connecting, and Communicating
- C. Technical, Troubleshooting, and Communication
- D. Time Management, Scheduling, and Documenting
- E. Practical, Analytical, and Methodological

C is the correct answer

Question ID: 14

Of the following, which four are among the top ten customer service expectations?

- A. Being given progress reports if a problem can't be fixed immediately.
- B. Being allowed to talk to someone in authority.
- C. Being dealt with fairly and objectively.
- D. Being contacted promptly when a problem is resolved.
- E. Being told about ways to prevent a future problem.

A, B, D, and E are the correct answers

Question ID: 15

Maintaining loyal customers is important because:

    A. It costs much more to acquire a new customer than to keep an existing one.

    B. Customer loyalty is the only measurement of your and your department's success.

    C. A loyal customer will cause fewer support problems.

    D. You can build a better rapport with a loyal customer.

    E. None of the above

A is the correct answer

Question ID: 16

Why is the communication skill set so important to successful support?

    A. You may need to justify the troubleshooting process.

    B. You have to be able to communicate your technical knowledge to demonstrate it.

    C. Customers respond better to technicians when they can converse with them.

    D. You will need to communicate with other people throughout the support process.

D is the correct answer

Question ID: 61

In addition to getting the problem fixed, customers measure service by how _____.

    A. the technician dressed

    B. fast the problem was fixed

    C. they were treated

    D. the competition advertises

C is the correct answer

Question ID: 62

The number one service expectation by customers is:

    A.   being called back when promised.
    B.   working with the same service rep.
    C.   fast problem resolution.
    D.   warrantied service calls.

A is the correct answer

THE CUSTOMER SERVICE ORGANIZATION

For review of this topic, refer to Chapter 2.

Question ID: 17

What is the main advantage of telephone help desk support?

    A.   It has relatively low overhead costs.
    B.   It provides support over a wide geographical area.
    C.   It allows quick and efficient classification of problems.
    D.   It allows for flexible support coverage.
    E.   The support personnel do not have to be as knowledgeable.

B is the correct answer

Question ID: 18

You are being put in charge of a new help desk support center. Which of the following are most important to organizing such a center?

    A.   Setting up an orderly workspace.
    B.   Establishing a structured escalation policy.
    C.   Reviewing customer-related documentation.
    D.   Maintaining an up-to-date list of personnel.
    E.   Requesting sufficient and appropriate office supplies and furniture.

A, B, and C are the correct answers

Question ID: 19

What is an important advantage of using a depot service center?

    A.   A dedicated support environment promotes greater technical expertise.
    B.   Drop-off servicing gives the technician greater flexibility in assigning priorities.
    C.   Centralized service and storage aids in preserving customer security.
    D.   A relatively small number of technicians can service a large number of systems.

D is the correct answer

Question ID: 20

What support needs can you effectively address in a help-desk environment?

    A. Gathering and recording of customer system information.

    B. Distribution of software and hardware FAQs.

    C. Gathering and analysis of marketing information.

    D. Explanations of the limits of the operating system.

    E. Recording of customer preferences for support personnel.

A is the correct answer

Question ID: 21

From your company's point of view, what is a potential bonus associated with field service support?

    A. Field service can serve as an excellent training ground for support personnel.

    B. Face-to-face communication leaves more opportunity for selling the product.

    C. After an initial service period, field service organizations will often charge for support.

    D. Problems that cannot be solved by a help desk can always be solved by a "house call."

C is the correct answer

Question ID: 22

What three elements are necessary to a structured escalation policy?

    A. A definition of major service outages.

    B. Establishment of parameters for automatic escalation.

    C. A known set of available problem-solving resources.

    D. Identification of a primary point of contact for both vendors and customers.

    E. Isolation of frequently escalated customers to special escalation tracks.

A, B, and D are the correct answers

Question ID: 57

Before contacting a customer, or going on site, it is important to review:

    A.   your performace measurement goals.

    B.   the technical manual.

    C.   any documentation already open on that call.

    D.   your customer's most recent stock quote.

C is the correct answer

Question ID: 74

A _____ work area will facilitate efficient customer support.

    A.   jumbled

    B.   neat

    C.   well-inventoried

    D.   busy

B and C are the correct answers

DIRECTIONAL TROUBLESHOOTING

For review of this topic, refer to Chapter 3.

Question ID: 23

The "D" in the DIReCtional model of troubleshooting stands for:

A. Define
B. Describe
C. Discover
D. Document

A is the correct answer

Question ID: 24

At what stage of the troubleshooting process should you take the time to document your progress?

A. Investigating the problem.
B. Isolating the problem.
C. Resolving the problem.
D. Closing the process.
E. Every stage.

E is the correct answer

Question ID: 25

When is an appropriate time to confirm a problem's identification with the customer?

A. After you believe you have isolated the problem.
B. When they ask; don't volunteer the information.
C. At least every day the problem is open.
D. When you need more information about the problem.
E. When you are finished fixing the problem in question.

A is the correct answer

Question ID: 26

What three purposes does documentation serve in the DIReCtional model of troubleshooting?

- A. It provides a history of problems with individual systems for future reference.
- B. It keeps track of what you have already tried in case another technician has to take over.
- C. It lets your supervisor know what you have been doing.
- D. It ensures that you can explain your course of action by making you write it down.
- E. It allows records on hardware and software problems to be analyzed for possible trends.

A, B, and E are the correct answers

Question ID: 27

Of the following questions, which two are relevant to isolating a problem as opposed to defining it?

- A. Can the problem be recreated?
- B. Is the problem a common occurrence?
- C. Where is the customer located?
- D. Is the customer on the network when the problem occurs?
- E. What time of day does the problem happen?

A and B are the correct answers

Question ID: 28

Defining a problem includes answering what questions?

- A. Where is the customer located?
- B. What time of day did the problem occur?
- C. In what physical environment is the customer's system located?
- D. How long has the customer been using computers?
- E. All of the above

A, B, and C are the correct answers

Question ID: 29

Which of the following can be useful sources of information for resolving problems?

A. Public library collections
B. Technicians at a software vendor
C. Local user groups
D. The Microsoft Web Page
E. Proprietary troubleshooting databases

B, C, and D are the correct answers

Question ID: 30

What is the last step in the DIReCtional process?

A. Communicating the solution to the customer.
B. Conferring with your fellow technicians.
C. Closing the problem report.
D. Confirming the resolution you reached.
E. Creating a document trail.

D is the correct answer

Question ID: 31

Of the following pieces of information, which four should you collect during the Definition phase of the DIReCtional model?

A. Type of Processor in problem system
B. Amount of RAM in problem system
C. Operating System running on problem system
D. Time of day that the problem occurred last.
E. Whether the problem can be reproduced on the user's system.

A, B, C, and D are the correct answers

Question ID: 32

Of the following, which four should you communicate back to the customer?

    A. The exact nature of the problem.
    B. What you did to solve the problem.
    C. Why the customer needs more training.
    D. How the customer might avoid the problem in the future.
    E. Why a problem cannot be resolved at the present time.

A, B, D, and E are the correct answers

Question ID: 33

For what reasons should you broadcast the problem and its solution to other technical support personnel and customers after its resolution?

    A. Your customer will want confirmation that you did what you said you did.
    B. You may be the only person in the organization who knows how to solve it.
    C. Your solution may affect future purchasing decisions.
    D. Your support organization will lose credibility if you don't.
    E. It may save your company time and money.

B, C, and E are the correct answers

Question ID: 34

Which phase of the DIReCtional model most helps to build customer confidence in you as a support professional?

    A. Quick response to problem calls.
    B. Technical expertise during troubleshooting.
    C. Confirmation of the problem and how it was solved.
    D. Accurate definition of the problem early in the process
    E. Masterful use of external and internal resources.

C is the correct answer

Question ID: 54

During the problem isolation troubleshooting phase, it is important to reconfirm the customer's _____ of the trouble situation.

    A. Understanding
    B. Trouble ticket number
    C. Frustration
    D. Staff involvement

A is the correct answer

Question ID: 55

When closing out the trouble call, part of the documentation procedures include:

    A. Sending an invoice to your client
    B. Reviewing the case history and results with your client
    C. Avoiding all paperwork
    D. A and B

B is the correct answer

Question ID: 59

When closing out the problem, in addition to reviewing the problem cause, it is important to identify _____ procedures to avoid future trouble occurences.

    A. Review
    B. Complex
    C. Two
    D. Maintenance

D is the correct answer

Question ID: 60

In addition to reviewing equipment related service bulletins or advisories with your customer during the service call, what other methods can you use to broadcast the information? (Choose two.)

A.   Radio announcement
B.   Intranet Web page
C.   Monthly newsletter
D.   Lunch room bulletin board

B and C are the correct answers

Question ID: 64

The first stage of the DIReCtional troubleshooting process enables you to:

A.   Finish your cup of coffee.
B.   Isolate the problem.
C.   Help your customer thoroughly describe the problem.
D.   Close out the trouble.

C is the correct answer

Question ID: 68

Intermittent problems require a coordinated partnership approach with your customer because they occur:

A.   All of the time.
B.   At inopportune moments.
C.   Infrequently.
D.   None of the above

C is the correct answer

COMMUNICATION SKILLS

For review of this topic, refer to Chapter 4.

Question ID: 35

Which of the following can be a detriment to effective listening skills?

    A. Putting yourself in the customer's position.

    B. Rehearsing your response to sound more professional.

    C. Visualizing them if they are speaking to you on the phone.

    D. Maintaining steady eye contact.

    E. Utilizing visual reinforcement to assure the customer of your attention.

B is the correct answer

Question ID: 36

What are reasons for using open-ended questions when talking to a customer?

    A. It allows the customer to contribute to the problem-solving process.

    B. It gives you time to work on the solution.

    C. It can provide vital detailed information.

    D. It lets the customer know that you are interested in the problem

    E. All of the above

A, C, and D are the correct answers

Question ID: 37

What is the first step of the ALERT process for dealing with a difficult situation?

    A. Ask the customer what the problem is.

    B. Allow the customer to say their piece.

    C. Apply your knowledge of communication skills.

    D. Acknowledge that the customer has a problem to solve.

    E. Answer any questions the customer has.

D is the correct answer

Question ID: 38

Which of the following represent a good application of reasonable expectations?

    A. Document your commitments and dates.

    B. Promise the customer immediate service.

    C. Treat your customer as a partner in the process.

    D. Assure the customer that you will be able to fix the problem.

    E. Build in a time "buffer" to allow for unexpected developments.

A, C, and E are the correct answers

Question ID: 39

What four activities below are part of a good "follow-up" to a problem?

    A. Making sure your customer is totally satisfied with the situation.

    B. Asking if your customer has any suggestions for improving your service.

    C. Updating customer records for future support reference.

    D. Asking if your customer could fix the problem without your help next time.

    E. Providing the customer with your calling card for their future use.

A, B, C, and E are the correct answers

Question ID: 40

What do phone and face-to-face listening techniques have in common?

    A. Thorough note-taking is important to prevent future confusion.

    B. Good posture allows you to present a positive image.

    C. Confirmation of what the customer says reassures them that you are paying attention.

    D. Avoiding listening to other conversations can prevent distractions.

A, C, and D are the correct answers

Question ID: 41

Closed-ended questions are effective tools for:

    A. Nothing. Use only open-ended questions to avoid offending the customer.

    B. Confirmation of information gained from open-ended questions.

    C. Quick gathering of detailed information from the beginning.

    D. Expanding the scope of the information-gathering process.

    E. Avoiding useless information from users not familiar with their equipment.

B is the correct answer

Question ID: 42

For what reasons is empathizing with the customer important?

    A. It helps you to understand why the problem is upsetting.

    B. It lets you understand how they do their job better.

    C. It prevents confusion about how the problem happened.

    D. It reminds you of how you would want to be treated in a similar situation.

A and D are the correct answers

Question ID: 49

The ability to listen actively and focus your attention on the customer shows your customer that you care and helps you to:

    A. stall instead of answering the question.

    B. gain valuable information.

    C. gain customer's trust.

    D. None of the above

B and C are the correct answers

Question ID: 51

Which type of questioning technique is best suited to probe for problem clarification?

A. Analytical
B. Multiple choice
C. Open-ended
D. Close-ended

C is the correct answer

Question ID: 53

Which of the following series of techniques demonstrate effective listening skills?

A. Maintain eye contact, positive body language, note taking
B. Interuptions, nodding, humming
C. Good eye contact, humming, following distractions
D. None of the above

A is the correct answer

Question ID: 56

When providing telephone support the phrases, "I understand" or "yes" signify:

A. You are not listening to your customer.
B. You are maintaining a peaceful conversation.
C. You have no idea what your customer means.
D. You are exercising verbal confirmation.

D is the correct answer

Question ID: 58

It is important to build in a _____ when you are setting a customer's expectations in order not to disappoint them.

    A.   Time buffer
    B.   Cash slush fund
    C.   Reliability factor
    D.   False promise

A is the correct answer

Question ID: 63

What must you do before drawing any conclusions regarding your customer's situation?

    A.   Interrupt their explanation.
    B.   Read the latest technical magazine.
    C.   Maintain eye contact.
    D.   Allow them to fully describe the situation.

D is the correct answer

Question ID: 65

Setting your customer's expectations is an important procedure because it enables you to focus your customer on those activities that _____ can be accomplished.

    A.   Realistically
    B.   Undoubtedly
    C.   Never
    D.   None of the above

A is the correct answer

Question ID: 66

When you are working with customers who do not have a strong technical base, it is important to:

   A.   Speak with a supervisor.
   B.   Expect them to keep up with you.
   C.   Speak clearly and clarify technical terminology.
   D.   Provide them a learner's guide.

C is the correct answer

Question ID: 67

Customers should be _____ regarding the status of unresolved problems such as delays in equipment delivery or repairs.

   A.   Informed
   B.   Avoided
   C.   Silenced
   D.   None of the above

A is the correct answer

Question ID: 69

Once you have listened to your customer and understand the full problem, it is most important to

   A.   Fill out all of the internal paperwork.
   B.   Respond immediately to the problem at hand.
   C.   Put the problem in queue and move on to the next call.
   D.   None of the above

B is the correct answer

Question ID: 70

Once you have made a promise to a customer, you _____ .

    A. Can renegotiate the commitment.
    B. Must deliver on the promise.
    C. Can delay the action, if it is only one day late.
    D. Can blame someone else for non-compliance.

B is the correct answer

Question ID: 71

Sometimes, events are out of your control, in which case you should provide your customer _____.

    A. A letter of apology.
    B. A full refund.
    C. A list of alternative actions.
    D. A and B

C is the correct answer

Question ID: 72

Your personal appearance should help to demonstrate a _____ attitude.

    A. Comfortable
    B. Professional
    C. Trendy
    D. Hard-working

B is the correct answer

Question ID: 73

When your customer is angry and rages at you, you should:

    A. Argue back if you know you're right.
    B. Hang up the phone.
    C. Listen and address the issues calmly.
    D. Take the criticism personally.

C is the correct answer

CUSTOMER INTERACTION SKILLS CASE SCENARIOS

For review of this topic, refer to Chapter 5.

Question ID: 43

Several systems in the marketing department have been acting "oddly" lately, according to the departmental secretary, Madeleine. As she is not comfortable with giving you more technical details over the phone, you decide to visit the department. When you arrive at the department, you see that a large sample neon sales display, complete with high-voltage transformers, has been installed near the systems in question, which turn out to have display and network communication difficulties. Before you start any other troubleshooting activities, you should:

A. Order shielded cable for the network adapters and monitors.

B. Move or disconnect the display yourself to save time.

C. Explain to Madeleine why you need to move either the display or the systems to fix the problem.

D. Move one of the systems to another location for testing.

E. Ask someone in the department to move the display or disconnect the display.

C is the correct answer

Question ID: 44

You provide on-site and remote support for a company with more than fifty remote users, mostly sales representatives. Margaret, a sales rep from the Portland office, left a message on your voice mail stating that she had not been able to get her e-mail for several days. Her tone was polite, but you know the sales reps depend on e-mail for product availability information on a daily basis. Following the DIReCtional model, which of the following should you do before you contact Margaret?

A. Track down and collect the e-mail sent to the sales reps over the past few days.

B. Contact other sales reps to see if they have had e-mail problems too.

C. Set up a system with the same hardware and software as the sales reps use.

D. Check with your peers to see if Margaret has a reputation for complaining about her computer.

E. None of the above-call Margaret immediately.

E is the correct answer

Question ID: 45

An angry manager named Phil calls you from shipping and receiving. He says that no one there can log in to their systems, that this is the third time in two weeks the stupid computers have kept them from getting any work done, and that the technicians haven't been able to fix anything. What can you do to calm him down and start the troubleshooting process?

A. Remind him that technicians are people too and that yelling at you will not fix the problem.

B. Tell him that you understand the importance of the problem, listen to what he has to say, and let him know that you understand how frustrated he must feel.

C. Tell him you are calling up the records on that problem and that you will call him back when you have looked at them

D. Get the name of the last technician who worked on the systems and tell Phil you will make sure it gets fixed this time.

E. Ask Phil to describe in detail exactly what happens when the users there attempt to log in.

B is the correct answer

Question ID: 46

Jim, a secretary in the legal department, reports that his internal CD-ROM unit is not working. If he places a disc in it, it closes normally and the light goes on, but he cannot access its contents. In talking to him, you discover that he only uses one disc on a regular basis, but that he uses it every day. What steps would you try first to isolate the problem?

A. Have Jim try a different disc in his CD-ROM drive.

B. Have Jim reboot his system and insert the disc again.

C. Have Jim try his disc in another system with a CD-ROM drive.

D. Have Jim reinstall the drivers for the CD-ROM.

E. Hook up an external CD-ROM drive to Jim's system.

A and C are the correct answers

Question ID: 47

Priscilla, one of the newer accountants in Payroll, had reported that she cannot sign on to the network anymore. Her system is running Windows 95 on a Novell v3.x network. You determine that she was fine until yesterday afternoon when another technician, Amy, worked on her system on a seemingly unrelated matter. She reports that Amy fixed that problem, but that she had the case open and thinks something may have gotten knocked loose. She doesn't see anything loose from the outside, however. Which question would you ask next to further define the nature of the problem?

A. Ask Priscilla if any cables are loose on the back of the system.
B. Ask Amy if the system was OK when she left it yesterday.
C. Ask Priscilla if Amy made any changes to the system files.
D. Ask Amy if Priscilla had talked to her about login problems yesterday.
E. Ask Priscilla if anyone else in Payroll is having similar problems.

E is the correct answer

Question ID: 48

You are working at the Help Desk when you get a frantic call from Emil in the Houston sales office. The display on his monitor has been gradually shrinking in both Windows 95 and in full-screen DOS displays, and now his entire Windows 95 desktop only occupies a third of the screen when he boots up. None of the adjusting knobs work, and he wants to run out to Circuit City and buy a new monitor. What is the first thing you would ask Emil to do in order to isolate the problem?

A. Check the monitor cable to make sure it is firmly attached to the system.
B. Check the display settings in Windows 95 to make sure he has the right driver selected.
C. Attach his monitor to another PC running Windows 95 to see if it works there.
D. Tell you if any new electrical equipment has recently been installed nearby.
E. Boot his PC into Windows 95 Safe Mode.

C is the correct answer

Navigating DOS and Windows v3.x

DISK OPERATING SYSTEM (DOS)

For review of this topic, refer to Chapter 1.

Question ID: 12

Which wildcard character is used to replace a single character in a search string?

    A. ?

    B. *

    C. #

    D. %

A is the correct answer

Question ID: 13

Which command is used to display the DOS system version running on a PC?

    A. DOS?

    B. SYS

    C. VER

    D. VERSYS

C is the correct answer

Question ID: 14

Which of the following commands can be used to rename a file without creating a duplicate file?

    A. MOVE

    B. RECOPY

    C. COPY

    D. NAME

A is the correct answer

Question ID: 15

Which command is used to change the text that displays on the screen before the blinking cursor?

- A. DISPLAY
- B. ECHO
- C. COMMAND
- D. PROMPT

D is the correct answer

Question ID: 16

The "DEL" command is the same as the _____ command.

- A. REMOVE
- B. RENAME
- C. ERASE
- D. EXIT

C is the correct answer

Question ID: 17

Which of these commands is the fastest method of preparing a diskette for re-use with new data?

- A. FORMAT C: /U
- B. FORMAT C: /S
- C. FORMAT A: /Q
- D. FORMAT A: /S

C is the correct answer

Question ID: 18

The double dots in "CD .." represent:

    A.   the current directory
    B.   the parent directory
    C.   the root directory
    D.   the directory one level below the current one

B is the correct answer

Question ID: 19

The command _____ enables you to verify which version of DOS is currently running.

    A.   VERSION
    B.   TYPE
    C.   VER
    D.   CUR

C is the correct answer

Question ID: 20

EMM386.EXE is loaded to:

    A.   automatically perform defrag.
    B.   simulate a hard drive using RAM.
    C.   manage Expanded memory.
    D.   extended memory reserves during power failure.

C is the correct answer

Question ID: 21

The ATTRIB command assigns which file characteristics? (Mark all that apply.)

    A. Archive

    B. Read-Only

    C. Write-Enable

    D. Hidden

A, B, and D are the correct answers

Question ID: 22

What will the following command do? ATTRIB +R *.TXT

    A. Remove the read-only attribute for all files with a TXT extension.

    B. Enables the read-only attribute for all files with a TXT extension.

    C. Moves all files with a TXT extension.

    D. Renames all files with a TXT extension.

B is the correct answer

Question ID: 23

Which of the following file attributes are valid DOS attributes? (Mark all that apply.)

    A. Bootable

    B. Read-Only

    C. Hidden

    D. Backed-up

B and C are the correct answers

Question ID: 24

The MOUSE.COM driver is usually loaded during the _____ file execution.

  A. AUTOEXEC.BAT
  B. CONFIG.SYS
  C. CONFIGURATION
  D. NETWORKED

A is the correct answer

Question ID: 25

You install an external floppy drive. Which device driver is required during installation?

  A. FLOPPY.SYS
  B. DRIVER.SYS
  C. SMARTDRV.EXE
  D. RAMDRIVE.SYS

B is the correct answer

Question ID: 26

FDISK is used to _____: (Select all that apply.)

  A. Format hard disks.
  B. Create Partitions.
  C. Delete Partitions.
  D. Manage logical drives.

B, C, and D are the correct answers

Question ID: 27

What DOS command is used to remark a line within the CONFIG.SYS file?

- A. REM
- B. DOC
- C. COM
- D. SET

A is the correct answer

Question ID: 28

Which device driver reduces power consumption during idle time?

- A. CONSERV.EXE
- B. SMARTDRV.EXE
- C. POWER.EXE
- D. INTERLNK.EXE

C is the correct answer

Question ID: 29

Which sequence of commands would you use to move all files in C:\OLDFILES to C:\NEWFILES? You will start in C:\OLDFILES.

- A. MOVE C:\OLDFILES\ \NEWFILES\
- B. MOVE C:\OLDFILES\ALL C:\NEWFILES\ALL
- C. MOVE *.* C:\NEWFILES\ALL
- D. MOVE *.* C:\NEWFILES\
- E. COPY *.* C:\NEWFILES\ /ERASE

D is the correct answer

Question ID: 30

Which of the following functions can the FORMAT command carry out?

    A.   Verifying the disk surface.

    B.   Creating the boot record.

    C.   Transferring the system files.

    D.   Creating the logical drive.

    E.   All of the above

A, B, and C are the correct answers

Question ID: 31

A user has accidentally deleted the contents of his C:\FRED directory. Following your instructions, he has not done anything with his system since he discovered the deletion. What command would you use to recover the deleted files?

    A.   UNFORMAT C:\FRED*.*

    B.   UNDELETE C:\

    C.   UNDELETE C:*.*

    D.   UNFORMAT C:\

    E.   None of the above

E is the correct answer

Question ID: 32

What is the command to display all system files in the current directory?

    A.   DIR *.SYS

    B.   ATTRIB *.*

    C.   CD *.SYS

    D.   ATTRIB *.SYS

    E.   DIR *.* /AS

E is the correct answer

Question ID: 33

Which of the commands below will transfer system files from a floppy drive to the hard drive, assuming the current directory is A:\?

   A. COPY A:*.SYS C:\
   B. SYS C:\
   C. SYS A:\ C:\DOS\
   D. COPY A:*.SYS C:\DOS
   E. SYS A:*.SYS C:\

B is the correct answer

Question ID: 34

Which of the following contains the proper order when running FDISK?

   A. Create logical drives, create extended partition, create primary partition.
   B. Create primary partition, create logical drives, create extended partition.
   C. Create extended partition, create logical drives, create primary partition.
   D. Create primary partition, create extended partition, create logical drives.
   E. Create logical drives, create primary partition, create extended partition.

D is the correct answer

Question ID: 35

What will the display show after you type in DATE?

   A. Current date is <date>
   B. Current date is <date>Current time is <time>
   C. Enter new date (dd-mm-yy)
   D. Current date is <date>Enter new date (mm-dd-yy)
   E. Enter new date (mm-dd-yyyy)

D is the correct answer

Question ID: 36

What command, when the current directory is C:\, will display all files in all subdirectories?

A. DIR C:*.* /ALL
B. DIR C:\ /SUB
C. DIR C:\ /S
D. DIR C:*.**.*
E. DIR ALL

C is the correct answer

Question ID: 37

The TREE command shows:

A. All directories and subdirectories in the current directory.
B. All directories, subdirectories and files in the current directory.
C. All directories and subdirectories on the disk.
D. All directories, subdirectories and files on the disk.
E. None of the above

A is the correct answer

Question ID: 38

Which command below would you use to prepare a floppy disk for use as a DOS system disk?

A. FORMAT A:\ /S
B. FORMAT A:\ /SYSTEM
C. FORMAT A:\ /BOOT
D. FORMAT A:\ /B
E. FORMAT C:\ A:\ /S

A is the correct answer

Question ID: 39

The FC (File Compare) command can be used to compare:

    A. Text files.
    B. Data files.
    C. Program files.
    D. All files except program files.
    E. All files.

E is the correct answer

Question ID: 40

In order to recover data lost after a FORMAT has been run on a disk, you must:

    A. Repartition the disk using FDISK.
    B. Run UNDELETE on the whole disk.
    C. Run UNFORMAT on the disk.
    D. Run CHKDSK /F on the disk.
    E. There is no way to recover data after a disk is formatted.

C is the correct answer

Question ID: 41

The current directory is C:\. Which of the following commands will make the C:\DOS directory hidden?

    A. ATTRIB C:\DOS*.* /H
    B. ATTRIB DOS /H
    C. ATTRIB C:\DOS /H
    D. ATTRIB DOS /AH
    E. None of the above

B and C are the correct answers

Question ID: 42

What utility will recover data after FDISK has been used to repartition a hard drive?

    A. UNFORMAT
    B. UNDELETE
    C. UNPARTITON
    D. UNFDISK
    E. There is no way of recovering data after the drive has been repartitioned.

E is the correct answer

Question ID: 43

One can often increase the amount of conventional memory available for running programs by:

    A. Loading devices in the CONFIG.SYS file into the Upper Memory area.
    B. Loading EMM386.EXE into the Upper Memory area.
    C. Loading the resident portion of DOS into the High Memory area.
    D. Loading TSRs in the AUTOEXEC.BAT file into the Upper Memory area.
    E. All of the above

A, C, and D are the correct answers

Question ID: 44

In order to move hidden files during disk optimization, you should use the following command:

    A. DEFRAG C: /MOVEALL
    B. DEFRAG C: /H
    C. DEFRAG C: /ALL
    D. DEFRAG will automatically move hidden files.
    E. DEFRAG cannot be made to move hidden files.

B is the correct answer

Question ID: 45

The high memory area is created when:

A. DOS-HIGH statement executes.
B. EMM386.SYS is loaded.
C. HIMEM.SYS is loaded.
D. More than 4 MB of memory is installed in the PC.

C is the correct answer

Question ID: 46

Which wildcard character is used to replace a combination of characters in a search string?

A. ?
B. %
C. *
D. #

C is the correct answer

Question ID: 47

Which of the following files is most likely to hold parameter information about a program?

A. XXXX.EXE
B. XXXX.INI
C. XXXX.SYS
D. XXXX.COM

B is the correct answer

Question ID: 48

What kind of information does a file with a .INI extension generally contain?

    A. Commands to be executed in succession.

    B. Batch commands.

    C. Instructions for the user.

    D. Parameter information about a program.

D is the correct answer

Question ID: 49

What commands are associated with the system clock? (Mark all that apply.)

    A. TIME

    B. CAL

    C. DATE

    D. SYSDATE

    E. SYSTIME

A and C are the correct answers

Question ID: 50

If the line FILES=30 was placed in CONFIG.SYS, what would be the result?

    A. When running Windows, you could have 3 applications and 27 files open at one time.

    B. Any number of files may be open, as long as the total combined file size does not exceed 30 MB.

    C. Any number of files may be open, as long as the total combined file size does not exceed 30 KB.

    D. A maximum of 30 files may be open at any given time.

D is the correct answer

Question ID: 51

The FILES command specifies:

    A. The number of files that can be open at one time.

    B. The number of different applications that may be open at one time.

    C. The number of files that may be placed in a directory.

    D. The total number of files that may be placed in a directory and its subdirectories.

A is the correct answer

Question ID: 52

Which of the following CONFIG.SYS commands is NOT valid?

    A. STACKS=9,256

    B. STACKS=0,0

    C. STACKS=7,0

    D. STACKS=8,32

C is the correct answer

Question ID: 53

In the CONFIG.SYS file, the command STACKS=9,256 means:

    A. 9,256 stacks of 64 Kbits each have been set aside for multitasking.

    B. 9 stacks of 256 KB have been set aside for DOS Kernel operations.

    C. 9 stacks of 256 KB have been set aside for disk buffering.

    D. 9 stacks of 256 bytes have been set aside for processing IRQs.

D is the correct answer

Question ID: 54

Which of the following commands would be placed in a CONFIG.SYS file?

    A. DEVICE=C:\DOS\HIMEM.SYS
    B. DEVICE=C:\DOS\HIMEM.EXE
    C. LOAD EXP160DI = HIGH
    D. SET TEMP=C:\DOS

A is the correct answer

Question ID: 55

What is the purpose of buffers?

    A. Allocate space in memory reserved for file and data transfer.
    B. Simulate a hard drive in memory.
    C. Create a disk cache in extended memory.
    D. Create a disk cache in expanded memory.

A is the correct answer

Question ID: 56

How many logical drives are possible when using DOS?

    A. 2
    B. 3
    C. 23
    D. Any number

C is the correct answer

Question ID: 57

Which of the following is a valid DOS filename? (Choose all that apply.)

- A. RE@CHEE.BAT
- B. SEPTEMBER.RPT
- C. TEST.123
- D. FILE1&2.DOC

A, C, and D are the correct answers

Question ID: 58

The default command prompt is established by placing the command PROMPT=PG in the ____ file.

- A. AUTOEXEC.BAT
- B. CONFIG.SYS
- C. COMMAND.COM
- D. SYSTEM.INI

A is the correct answer

Question ID: 59

To start the computer, the DOS system files must be in the _____, _____ partition.

- A. extended, active
- B. primary, active
- C. primary, logical
- D. primary, initial
- E. extended, initial

B is the correct answer

Question ID: 60

What is the largest partition size available for DOS v6.0?

A. 32 MB
B. 100 MB
C. 1 GB
D. 2 GB

D is the correct answer

Question ID: 61

What is the order of execution for the startup files?

A. CONFIG.SYS, then AUTOEXEC.BAT
B. AUTOEXEC.BAT, then CONFIG.SYS
C. CONFIG.SYS, AUTOEXEC.BAT, then SMARTDRV
D. CONFIG.SYS, MEMMAKER, then AUTOEXEC.BAT

A is the correct answer

Question ID: 62

What was the first operating system developed for IBM PCs and compatibles?

A. IBM-DOS
B. DOS
C. OS/2
D. MVS

B is the correct answer

Question ID: 63

The first 640 KB of system memory is called:

- A. Conventional Memory.
- B. Upper Memory Area (UMA).
- C. Standard Memory.
- D. Extended Memory.

A is the correct answer

Question ID: 64

What is the first 64 KB of memory above 1 MB called?

- A. Extended Memory (XMS).
- B. High Memory Area (HMA).
- C. Expanded Memory (EMS).
- D. Upper Memory Area (UMA).

B is the correct answer

Question ID: 65

_____ is the system of organizing electronic files in directories, subdirectories and individual files.

- A. A file cabinet structure
- B. Standard business organization
- C. The Gregg filing system
- D. A directory tree

D is the correct answer

Question ID: 66

If a PC freezes during boot, you should reboot and press _____ when the message "Starting DOS..." appears to bypass the startup files.

    A. Escape <Esc> and F1
    B. Escape <Esc> and F5
    C. F1
    D. F5

D is the correct answer

Question ID: 67

The PIF editor manages _____ and is located in the Main program group.

    A. Customized icons.
    B. DOS-based applications.
    C. Clipboard entries.
    D. File and directory structure.

B is the correct answer

Question ID: 68

Pressing the F8 key during the boot process will enable you to:

    A. Deny access to CONFIG.SYS.
    B. Deny access to AUTOEXEC.BAT.
    C. Insert custom startup commands.
    D. Selectively bypass CONFIG.SYS and AUTOEXEC.BAT commands.

D is the correct answer

Question ID: 69

Which of the following are not DOS operating system boot files?

    A. IO.SYS
    B. MSDOS.SYS
    C. HIMEM.SYS
    D. COMMAND.COM

C is the correct answer

Question ID: 70

An operating system enables:

    A. Interaction between the system board and add-ons.
    B. Interaction between applications and data.
    C. Interaction between the user and PC hardware.
    D. Interaction between software and developers.

C is the correct answer

Question ID: 71

Which of the following are system files required for DOS to boot up a computer?

    A. IO.SYS
    B. MSDOS.SYS
    C. BOOTLOG.COM
    D. COMMAND.COM
    E. USER.COM

A, B, and D are the correct answers

Question ID: 72

A directory inside a subdirectory is called a _____.

    A.   Subsubdirectory

    B.   File

    C.   Folder

    D.   Subdirectory

    E.   Underdirectory

D is the correct answer

Question ID: 73

Which of the following are legal filenames in DOS?

    A.   LPT1.EXE

    B.   GOODNAME.D??

    C.   BAD!NAME.DOC

    D.   .ILLEGAL.DOC

    E.   All of the above

C is the correct answer

Question ID: 74

Which of the following are legal filenames in DOS?

    A.   FILENAME2

    B.   FILENAM!.DOC

    C.   FILENAM>.EXE

    D.   FILENAME.233

B and D are the correct answers

Question ID: 166

Using the DIR command in your C:\DATAFILE directory causes the screen to scroll by too quickly to read. As a result, you only see a handful of files, the total number of files (4,337), and their total size (45,334,100 bytes) at the bottom of the listing. How might you more effectively view the contents of the directory and information on them?

    A. Use DIR with the /W switch to use the wide format directory display.

    B. Use DIR with the /P switch to view the contents one screen at a time.

    C. Use DIR with the /S switch to view the contents one screen at a time.

    D. Use DIR with the /O switch to activate the other view menu.

    E. Use TREE instead of DIR.

B is the correct answer

SYSTEM OPTIMIZATION UNDER DOS

For review of this topic, refer to Chapter 2.

Question ID: 75

The MS-DOS utility SCANDISK:

    A. Rearranges non-contiguous files into contiguous files.
    B. Finds lost allocation units and gives you the option of discarding or saving them.
    C. Rearranges programs in upper memory to optimize utilization.
    D. Displays the amount of free conventional memory.

B is the correct answer

Question ID: 76

The DEFRAG utility in MS-DOS:

    A. Rearranges non-contiguous files into contiguous files.
    B. Finds lost allocation units and gives you the option of discarding or saving them.
    C. Rearranges programs in upper memory to optimize utilization.
    D. Displays the amount of free conventional memory.

A is the correct answer

Question ID: 77

The program, SMARTDRV.EXE _____.

    A. Creates a disk cache in extended memory.
    B. Creates a disk cache in expanded memory.
    C. Simulates a hard drive in memory.
    D. Loads BIOS instructions into an IDE Drive.

A is the correct answer

Question ID: 78

Which of the following commands should the user run to view memory usage before using a memory optimizing program?

    A. RAMSETUP.EXE

    B. MEM

    C. MEMMAKER

    D. QMEM

B is the correct answer

Question ID: 79

To run RAMBoost, you need:

    A. A PC with a VESA Local Bus.

    B. A memory manager.

    C. An 80486DX2 or later chip.

    D. At least 640 KB memory on a IBM PC XT.

B is the correct answer

Question ID: 80

_____ was developed as a way of working around the limitations of DOS and early microprocessors.

    A. Upper Memory Area (UMA)

    B. Upper Memory Blocks (UMB)

    C. Extended Memory (XMS)

    D. Expanded Memory (EMS)

D is the correct answer

Question ID: 81

What is required to give access to expanded memory and the high memory area? (Mark all that apply.)

- A. A "LOADHIGH" statement must be placed in the CONFIG.SYS file.
- B. The command DEVICE=C:\DOS\HIMEM.SYS must be added to the AUTOEXEC.BAT file.
- C. A memory manager such as HIMEM.SYS must be loaded.
- D. An expanded memory manager must be loaded.

C and D are the correct answers

Question ID: 82

Which of the following commands creates a boot diskette?

- A. FORMAT A:/U /Q
- B. FORMAT A:/B
- C. FORMAT A:/S
- D. FORMAT A:/R /B

C is the correct answer

Question ID: 83

A surface scan reads every sector on the disk to verify that it is _____.

- A. Mapped
- B. Clustered
- C. Organized
- D. Readable

D is the correct answer

Question ID: 84

The ROM BIOS and video controller ROM reside in:

    A. Conventional Memory.

    B. The Upper Memory area.

    C. The High Memory area.

    D. Extended Memory.

    E. Expanded Memory.

B is the correct answer

Question ID: 85

You type in the command MEM /F /P. What will be displayed?

    A. Locations in memory of all running programs, page by page.

    B. Locations in memory of all free memory areas and page frames.

    C. Locations in memory of all running programs.

    D. Locations in memory of all free memory areas, page by page.

    E. Locations in memory of all page frames.

D is the correct answer

Question ID: 86

What line should you include in the CONFIG.SYS file to prevent interruption by the break (Crtl-C) command?

    A. NOBREAK

    B. CONTINUOUS=ON

    C. BREAK=OFF

    D. Interruption by the break command cannot be disabled in system files.

    E. Interruption by the break command is automatically disabled in system files.

C is the correct answer

Question ID: 87

SMARTDrive (SMARTDRV) serves what valuable purpose that can improve system performance?

- A. It keeps a record of the location of all recently used files for quicker disk access.
- B. It enables a data cache to speed up disk reads and writes.
- C. It automatically defragments the hard drive during normal use.
- D. It prevents the drive heads from attempting to read sectors outside the formatted area.
- E. It allows an area of memory to serve temporarily as a simulated hard drive.

B is the correct answer

Question ID: 88

A typical mouse installation in DOS:

- A. Requires that C:\MOUSE\MOUSE.COM be loaded in the AUTOEXEC.BAT file.
- B. Requires that DEVICE=C:\MOUSE\MOUSE.SYS be loaded in the CONFIG.SYS file.
- C. Requires that C:\MOUSE\MOUSE.COM be loaded in the AUTOEXEC.BAT file OR that DEVICE=C:\MOUSE\MOUSE.SYS be loaded in the CONFIG.SYS file, but not both.
- D. Requires that C:\MOUSE\MOUSE.COM be loaded in the AUTOEXEC.BAT file AND that DEVICE=C:\MOUSE\MOUSE.SYS be loaded in the CONFIG.SYS file.

C is the correct answer

Question ID: 89

MEMMAKER, when run in Custom mode, allows you to:

    A.   Optimize high memory use by Windows.

    B.   Keep currently defined EMM386.EXE inclusions and exclusions.

    C.   Scan high memory aggressively.

    D.   Use the video color display area for running programs.

    E.   All of the above

B is the correct answer

Question ID: 90

The /HMAMIN=m switch in HIMEM.SYS controls what?

    A.   The amount of memory in KB to be made available in the High Memory area (default is all).

    B.   The number of times HIMEM will run its memory test routine (default is 1).

    C.   The amount of memory in KB that a program must need before it can access the High Memory area (default is 0).

    D.   The amount of memory in KB reserved in the High Memory area for DOS (default is 64 KB).

    E.   The amount of memory in KB the High Memory controller can access (default is all).

C is the correct answer

Question ID: 91

Which two of the following parameters normally appear in the AUTOEXEC.BAT file?

    A.   PROMPT=pg

    B.   SET Temp=C:\TEMP

    C.   FCBS=16

    D.   FILES=50

    E.   BUFFERS=16

A and B are the correct answers

Question ID: 92

In order to run SCANDISK on a floppy drive while fixing errors, saving lost clusters as files, and executing a surface scan, which of the following command strings would you use to avoid needing user interaction?

A. SCANDISK A: /AUTOFIX /NOSUMMARY /SAVE /SURFACE
B. SCANDISK A: /AUTOALL /SURFACE
C. SCANDISK A: /AUTOFIX /NOSUMMARY /SURFACE
D. SCANDISK A: /FIXERRORS /SAVEFILES /SURFACE
E. SCANDISK A: /AUTOFIX /NOSAVE /SURFACE

C is the correct answer

Question ID: 93

Which of the following commands will free up the most conventional memory?

A. DOS=HIGH
B. DOS=UMB
C. DOS=LOW,UMB
D. DOS=HIGH,UMB
E. DOS=HIGH,NOUMB

D is the correct answer

Question ID: 94

What will be the result of placing the following line in the CONFIG.SYS file?
DEVICE=C:\DOS\EMM386.EXE X=C000-CFFF WIN=C000-CCFF

A. The memory address range CD00-CFFF will be excluded and the memory address range C000-CCFF will be reserved for Windows operations.
B. The memory address range C000-CFFF will be excluded.
C. The memory address range C000-CCFF will be reserved for Windows operation.
D. An error message will be returned and the system may hang.
E. The line will be ignored.

B is the correct answer

Question ID: 95

If a device driver is loaded high in the CONFIG.SYS file, but no upper memory is available, what will happen?

A. The device driver will be loaded into high memory.
B. The device driver will be loaded into conventional memory.
C. The device driver will not be loaded.
D. The system will hang.
E. The device driver will load into extended memory.

B is the correct answer

Question ID: 96

Disabling virtual memory on a system with over 32 MB of RAM can:

A. Actually speed up the processing of large data files.
B. Cause problems running multiple applications.
C. Force the system to create a shadowed swap file.
D. Cause data to be overwritten by Windows startup.
E. Slow down DOS session activity in Windows.

B is the correct answer

Question ID: 167

You wish to enable upper memory access without expanded memory support. Your system has an Ethernet card that requires memory addresses D000h-D800h and DC00h-DFFFh to be reversed. Which command below should you use in the CONFIG.SYS file to accomplish these goals?

A. DEVICE=C:\DOS\EMM386.EXE RAM X=D000-D800 X=DC00-DFFF
B. DEVICE=C:\DOS\EMM386.EXE NOEMS I=D000-DFFF
C. DEVICE=C:\DOS\EMM386.EXE XMS X=D000-D800 X=DC00-DFFF
D. DEVICE=C:\DOS\EMM386.EXE NOEMS X=D000-D800 X=DC00-DFFF
E. DEVICE=C:\DOS\EMM386.EXE NOEMS ROM=D000-D800 ROM=DC00-DFFF

D is the correct answer

WINDOWS V3.1

For review of this topic, refer to Chapter 3.

Question ID: 97

Which of the following is NOT a valid Windows system initialization file?

    A. WIN.INI
    B. SYS.INI
    C. PROGMAN.INI
    D. WINFILE.INI

B is the correct answer

Question ID: 98

Which .INI files are most likely to require editing? (Mark all that apply.)

    A. SYSTEM.INI
    B. SETUP.INI
    C. PROGMAN.INI
    D. WIN.INI

A and D are the correct answers

Question ID: 99

Which of the following files can be edited with SYEDIT, the Windows System Editor? (Mark all that apply)

    A. AUTOEXEC.BAT
    B. CONTROL.INI
    C. CONFIG.SYS
    D. SYSTEM.INI
    E. SYS.INI

A, C, and D are the correct answers

Question ID: 100

What is a PIF?

    A.   Program Initialization File

    B.   Program Information File

    C.   Programmable Init File

    D.   Program Information Font

B is the correct answer

Question ID: 101

Which of the following statements best describes Windows? (Mark all that apply.)

    A.   Windows is an operating system that works in conjunction with DOS.

    B.   Windows is a graphical user interface.

    C.   Real-mode operations allow Windows to run on 80286 CPUs.

    D.   Windows provides multitasking capabilities.

B and D are the correct answers

Question ID: 102

Windows 3.1 no longer supports:

    A.   Real-mode operations.

    B.   Standard-mode operations.

    C.   386 Enhanced-mode operations.

    D.   Custom setup.

A is the correct answer

Question ID: 103

Which of the following files will affect Windows performance? (Mark all that apply.)

A. AUTOEXEC.BAT
B. COMMAND.COM
C. CONFIG.SYS
D. DOS Kernel

A, C, and D are the correct answers

Question ID: 104

Which is the loader file that launches Windows?

A. WIN.INI
B. WIN.SYS
C. WIN.COM
D. WIN.CNF

C is the correct answer

Question ID: 105

Windows verifies that an extended memory (XMS) driver such as HIMEM.SYS, QEMM, or 386-Max is present when _____ executes.

A. WIN.CNF
B. WIN.COM
C. WIN.EXE
D. WIN.INI

B is the correct answer

Question ID: 106

Which of the following is a Windows core component file?

A. USER.INI
B. KERNL286.EXE
C. GDI.EXE
D. SYSTEM.INI

C is the correct answer

Question ID: 107

What is the function of the WIN.INI file?

A. Contains color schemes, patterns, printer settings, and installable driver settings.
B. Contains system hardware setting information.
C. Controls Windows environmental settings.
D. Defines the appearance and actions of File Manager components and objects.

C is the correct answer

Question ID: 108

What is the function of the SYSTEM.INI file?

A. Controls Windows environmental settings.
B. Contains system hardware setting information.
C. Defines the appearance and actions of File Manager components and objects.
D. Contains color schemes, patterns, printer settings and installable driver settings.

B is the correct answer

Question ID: 109

What is the function of the CONTROL.INI file?

A. Controls Windows environmental settings.
B. Contains system hardware setting information.
C. Defines the appearance and actions of File Manager components and objects.
D. Contains color schemes, patterns, printer settings, and installable driver settings.

D is the correct answer

Question ID: 110

_____ defines Program Manager information, such as the location of .GRP files and the size and location of the Program Manager window.

    A. WIN.INI

    B. CONTROL.INI

    C. PROGMAN.INI

    D. WINFILE.INI

C is the correct answer

Question ID: 111

What type of font is stored as a bitmap?

    A. TrueType

    B. Raster

    C. Printer

    D. PostScript

B is the correct answer

Question ID: 112

What type of font is defined as a mathematical model?

    A. ASCII

    B. Raster

    C. Vector

    D. PostScript

C is the correct answer

Question ID: 113

What is the purpose of a program group file?

    A. It contains information for creating a programs user interface.
    B. It contains information about the icons included in the program group.
    C. It launches executable programs.
    D. They contain information about environmental requirements of similar programs.

B is the correct answer

Question ID: 114

What extension is normally used on sound files?

    A. .SND
    B. .SRC
    C. .ECO
    D. .WAV

D is the correct answer

Question ID: 115

_____ is a type of multitasking where the foreground application is active and the background applications are suspended.

    A. Task switching
    B. Cooperative multitasking
    C. Preemptive multitasking
    D. Terminate-Stay-Resident

A is the correct answer

Question ID: 116

_____ is a type of multitasking where the amount of time given to each application is based on each application's activity level.

 A. Task switching
 B. Cooperative multitasking
 C. Preemptive multitasking
 D. Active matrix multitasking

B is the correct answer

Question ID: 117

_____ is a type of multitasking that allocates equal slices of time to each open application.

 A. Task switching
 B. Cooperative multitasking
 C. Preemptive multitasking
 D. Passive task switching

C is the correct answer

Question ID: 118

Which of the following commands will start Windows without displaying the Microsoft Windows logo?

 A. WIN /R
 B. WIN /2
 C. WIN /S
 D. WIN :

D is the correct answer

Question ID: 119

Which of the following commands will force Windows to start in the Standard mode?

    A. WIN /R
    B. WIN /2
    C. WIN /S
    D. WIN /3

C is the correct answer

Question ID: 120

Virtual Memory is best described as:

    A. A RAM cache reserved in the high memory area that can be used by programs.
    B. A file on the hard disk that emulates physical RAM.
    C. A RAM cache reserved in the extended memory area that can be used by programs.
    D. A RAM cache reserved in the expanded memory area that can be used by programs.

B is the correct answer

Question ID: 121

The purpose of a Program Information File (PIF) is to:

    A. Define the requirements for DOS applications.
    B. Initialize files in a Windows environment.
    C. Reconfigure the system as required when a DOS application is launched in Windows.
    D. Select the printer driver required by different programs.

A is the correct answer

Question ID: 122

Which of the following DOS commands should NOT be run in a DOS session in Windows? (Mark all that apply.)

A. CHKDSK
B. FDISK
C. CHKDSK /F
D. Formatting a floppy drive

B and C are the correct answers

Question ID: 123

Which of the following drivers will support CD-ROM access from a Windows environment.

A. RAMBOOST
B. MEMMAKER
C. MSCDEX
D. MSAV

C is the correct answer

Question ID: 124

Where are the program group filenames stored?

A. PROGMAN.PIF
B. PROGMAN.GRP
C. LISTING.INI
D. PROGMAN.INI

D is the correct answer

Question ID: 125

Two of the default program manager groups are: (Choose two.)

A. Main
B. Progman
C. Icon
D. Applications

A and D are the correct answers

Question ID: 126

.GRP files contain information for:

A. Screen Paintings
B. Program manager groups
C. Security logs
D. Passwords

B is the correct answer

Question ID: 127

Before making changes to the SYSTEM.INI file you should:

A. Verify hardware configuration.
B. Backup the original settings.
C. Reinstall Windows.
D. Run Defrag.

B is the correct answer

Question ID: 128

In a Windows environment, executable programs are represented as:

A. PIF files
B. Icons
C. Pull down menus
D. Program groups

B is the correct answer

Question ID: 129

The Windows operating environment includes which types of files?

    A.   INI files
    B.   DLL files
    C.   Core Component files
    D.   SCR files
    E.   All of the above

E is the correct answer

Question ID: 130

Features of the Windows v3.1 environment include:

    A.   A Graphical User Interface.
    B.   True 32-bit Multitasking.
    C.   Tunable performance.
    D.   C2 File System Security.
    E.   All of the above

A and C are the correct answers

Question ID: 131

As a rule, Virtual Device Drivers are specified in the _____ file.

    A.   WIN.INI
    B.   SYSTEM.INI
    C.   CONTROL.INI
    D.   USER.EXE
    E.   PROGMAN.INI

B is the correct answer

Question ID: 132

386 Enhanced Mode Windows is:

   A. Generally faster than Standard Mode Windows, due to the increased swapfile size.

   B. Sometimes slower than Standard Mode Windows, but not generally at a noticeable level.

   C. Much slower than Standard Mode Windows, due to the increased system load of the DOS virtual machines.

   D. Much faster than Standard Mode Windows, because of the EMS emulation.

   E. Totally indistinguishable in performance from Standard Mode Windows.

B is the correct answer

Question ID: 133

Windows supports the following types of fonts:

   A. Raster fonts.

   B. Vector fonts.

   C. Printer fonts.

   D. TrueType fonts.

   E. All of the above

E is the correct answer

Question ID: 134

The SYSTEM.INI file contains:

   A. Parameters required for Windows startup.

   B. Textual descriptions for Windows device drivers.

   C. Hexadecimal descriptions for Windows virtual device drivers.

   D. Settings for keyboard support.

   E. All of the above

A, B, and D are the correct answers

Question ID: 135

In 386 Enhanced mode, DOS sessions:

    A. Can only be run in full-screen mode.

    B. Inherit the DOS environment active when Windows was launched.

    C. Take up a minimum of 64 KB of conventional memory each.

    D. Cannot run in the background.

    E. Can run all DOS commands without any problems.

B is the correct answer

Question ID: 136

Installable multimedia drivers are listed in the _____ file.

    A. SYSTEM.INI

    B. WIN.INI

    C. CONTROL.INI

    D. DRIVERS.INI

    E. PROGMAN.INI

C is the correct answer

Question ID: 137

What is the minimum amount of free extended memory that must be available in order to install Windows to use 386 Enhanced Mode?

    A. 256 KB

    B. 312 KB

    C. 512 KB

    D. 1024 KB

D is the correct answer

Question ID: 138

In order to install Windows, what is the minimum setting for FILES= in the CONFIG.SYS?

    A. 20
    B. 30
    C. 40
    D. 50

B is the correct answer

Question ID: 139

Which SETUP option will install a shared copy of Windows on the network?

    A. /A
    B. /NET
    C. /N
    D. /O:net
    E. /B

A is the correct answer

Question ID: 140

If a device does not have a standard Windows device driver:

    A. Use a standard Windows device driver that approximates the device that you are installing.
    B. Use a Windows default device driver to approximate the needed device driver.
    C. Use the device driver supplied by the manufacturer.
    D. Do not install the device because it is not Windows compatible.

C is the correct answer

Question ID: 141

When installing Windows to run in Standard mode, what is the minimum CPU requirement?

A. An 8086 or faster processor.

B. An 80286 or faster processor.

C. An 80386 (SX) or faster processor.

D. An 80386 processor running at 16 MHz or faster.

B is the correct answer

Question ID: 142

What is the minimum processor required to run Windows in the Enhanced mode?

A. An 80386(DX) or faster processor.

B. An 80286 or faster processor.

C. An 80386(SX) or faster processor.

D. An 80486 or faster processor.

C is the correct answer

Question ID: 143

386 Enhanced mode requires at least _____ of XMS memory.

A. 1 MB

B. 2 MB

C. 4 MB

D. 8 MB

A is the correct answer

Question ID: 144

For Windows to recognize a serial mouse, on which COM ports can you install it?

    A. COM1 and COM3
    B. COM2 and COM4
    C. COM1 and COM2
    D. COM3 and COM4

C is the correct answer

Question ID: 145

Windows Setup can be run using which of the following options?

    A. Express setup
    B. Custom setup
    C. Automated setup
    D. All of the above

D is the correct answer

Question ID: 146

Before running setup, you should:

    A. Reformat the hard drive.
    B. Verify prerequisite hardware is installed.
    C. Back up all data.
    D. Organize the directory structure.

B is the correct answer

Question ID: 147

If you think you may have Windows-incompatible programs on your hard drive, you should use what command to set up Windows?

A.   SETUP /CHKDSK
B.   SETUP /I
C.   SETUP /T
D.   SETUP /C:
E.   SETUP /FIND

C is the correct answer

Question ID: 148

Which of the following are required for Windows installation?

A.   200 MB of hard drive space
B.   DOS v3.10 or higher
C.   384 KB of unused conventional memory
D.   A serial mouse on COM1
E.   All of the above

B and C are the correct answers

Question ID: 149

Custom Setup allows you to control which four of the following?

A.   Virtual memory settings
B.   Modifications to CONFIG.SYS and AUTOEXEC.BAT
C.   Hard drive space allotted to Windows setup files
D.   Whether existing applications are installed in Windows
E.   Video display settings

A, B, D, and E are the correct answers

Question ID: 150

When a Permanent Swap File is created: (Mark all that apply.)

    A. SPART.PAR is created.

    B. WIN386.SWP is created.

    C. 386SPART.SWP is created.

    D. 386SPART.PAR is created.

A and D are the correct answers

Question ID: 151

When a Temporary Swap File is created: (Mark all that apply.)

    A. SPART.PAR is created.

    B. WIN386.SWP is created.

    C. WIN386.PAR is created.

    D. 386SPART.PAR is created.

B is the correct answer

Question ID: 152

Which of the following will provide the best virtual memory performance?

    A. Setting the "MaxPagingFileSize=" equal to 16,866 or greater

    B. Creating a temporary swap file

    C. Setting "STACKS=9,256" in the CONFIG.SYS file

    D. Creating a permanent swap file

D is the correct answer

Question ID: 153

Which of the following statements about temporary swap files is correct?

A. A temporary swap file cannot be created on a redirected local area network drive.

B. A temporary swap file supports hard disks too fragmented for the creation of a permanent swap file.

C. A temporary swap file is fixed in size and cannot change size as necessary.

D. A temporary swap file is rather limited, providing virtual memory on a limited number of machines.

B is the correct answer

Question ID: 154

What must occur in order for changes to INI files to take effect?

A. Windows must be restarted.

B. The system must be rebooted.

C. No action is required.

D. Edit existing files.

A is the correct answer

Question ID: 155

_____ information is contained in the CONTROL.INI file.

A. Peripheral hardware

B. CONFIG.SYS

C. Visual screen appearance

D. Program Manager

C is the correct answer

Question ID: 156

Virtual memory support is provided:

    A. By 386 Enhanced Mode Windows only with 8 MB of RAM or greater.

    B. By Standard Mode Windows only with disk caching.

    C. By 386 Enhanced Mode Windows, if activated.

    D. By both Standard and 386 Mode Windows in all cases.

C is the correct answer

Question ID: 157

A GPF (General Protection Fault) is always the result of:

    A. Software incompatibility.

    B. A corrupt swap file.

    C. Hardware incompatibility.

    D. Memory conflicts.

    E. Inappropriate hard disk formatting.

D is the correct answer

Question ID: 158

Virtual Memory Management allows:

    A. The use of hard drive space as simulated RAM.

    B. The use of larger data files.

    C. A larger number of applications to be opened concurrently.

    D. Faster performance by most applications.

    E. All of the above

A, B, and C are the correct answers

Question ID: 159

The advantages of making custom PIFs for DOS-based applications in Windows include which four of the following?

A. The ability to tailor the memory requirements for the application.
B. The ability to choose full-screen or windowed display options.
C. The ability to select exclusive or background execution.
D. The ability to change swap file sizes and types "on the fly."
E. The ability to use the High Memory area.

A, B, C, and E are the correct answers

Question ID: 160

Which three of the following statements concerning swap files are true?

A. A permanent swap file usually provides faster performance than a temporary swap file.
B. A temporary swap file cannot be placed on a network drive.
C. A temporary swap file requires at least 4 MB of hard drive space.
D. A permanent swap file can be no larger than the largest contiguous block of free space on a hard drive.
E. A temporary swap file is deleted when you exit Windows.

A, D, and E are the correct answers

Question ID: 161

The BOOTLOG.TXT file created by the WIN /B command includes:

A. The support files called by WIN.COM and whether they loaded successfully.
B. The memory addresses used by USER.EXE on Windows startup.
C. The condition of any temporary swap files on local hard drives.
D. The paging status of any extended memory called by EMMWIN.EXE.
E. None of the above

A is the correct answer

Question ID: 162

DOS-based applications can be run in Windows by:

    A. Typing them into the command prompt line in a DOS session.
    B. Associating them with a type of data file and selecting the data file.
    C. Selecting them in File Manager.
    D. Setting up a PIF for the application and selecting it.
    E. All of the above

E is the correct answer

Question ID: 163

For print jobs in Windows to spool properly, they require:

    A. A temporary or permanent swap file of at least 4 MB.
    B. A SPOOL=ON statement in the WIN.INI file.
    C. Sufficient hard drive space for the job to be spooled to the TEMP directory.
    D. Sufficient expanded memory for the job to be spooled to the excluded Windows memory range there.
    E. A PostScript-compatible printer.

C is the correct answer

Question ID: 164

Which of the following is likely to improve performance on a Windows system that is slowing down with time?

    A. Increase the amount of conventional memory available using MEMMAKER or by manually loading drivers and TSRs into upper memory.
    B. Increasing the size of the swap file.
    C. Defragmenting the hard drive that contains the Windows directory.
    D. Compacting the hard drive that contains the Windows directory.
    E. All of the above

A, B, and C are the correct answers

Question ID: 168

Which of the following statements about troubleshooting are true?

A. Good, reliable, and recent backups are your best guarantee of recovering critical files.
B. Check for obvious possibilities, such as loose cables and power cords that are unplugged.
C. Feedback from the user is usually unreliable and can often be misleading.
D. It is wise to check for things that have changed, such as configuration settings or software upgrades.

A, B, and D are the correct answers

Question ID: 170

An important part of both ongoing management and troubleshooting is information. Which of the following types of information can assist you during the troubleshooting process?

A. System Inventory
B. System Files
C. Data Files
D. Error Messages

A, B, and D are the correct answers

Question ID: 171

Windows Setup places MSD.EXE in which directory?

A. C:\
B. C:\DOS
C. C:\WINDOWS
D. C:\WINDOWS\DIAGS

B is the correct answer

Question ID: 172

Of the following choices, which are types of information provided by running MSD.EXE?

   A. Computer

   B. Video

   C. Network

   D. User

A, B, and C are the correct answers

Question ID: 173

For troubleshooting purposes, you need to create a bootable diskette. Which of the following commands would you use?

   A. BOOTDISK.EXE

   B. CHKDISK.EXE

   C. FORMAT A: /B

   D. FORMAT A: /S

D is the correct answer

Question ID: 174

Joan's Windows 3.1 machine will not start in Standard mode. Which of the following steps will you take to troubleshoot this problem?

   A. Look for any changes that have been made to the system.

   B. Verify there is sufficient memory.

   C. Try booting with a Clean Boot Diskette.

   D. Try booting in 386 Enhanced mode.

A, B, and C are the correct answers

Question ID: 175

Which of the following statements are true about Windows and memory?

    A. In 386 Enhanced mode, the conventional memory environment at the time when Windows is launched is copied into each DOS session.

    B. In Standard mode, the conventional memory environment at the time when Windows is launched is copied into each DOS session.

    C. 386 Enhanced mode supports emulated EMS memory.

    D. Conventional memory and XMS memory are treated as one contiguous memory block.

A, C, and D are the correct answers

Question ID: 176

Which files make up the Windows 3.1 permanent swap file?

    A. SPART.PAR

    B. PART.PAR

    C. 386PART.PAR

    D. 386SPART.PAR

A and D are the correct answers

Question ID: 177

You receive an "Incorrect DOS Version" error. This message relates to a problem with which file?

    A. DOS.VER

    B. COMMAND.COM

    C. AUTOEXEC.BAT

    D. MSDOS.SYS

B is the correct answer

Question ID: 178

Which of the following statements about GPFs are true?

    A. A GPF occurs when Windows attempts to use a hardware device that it doesn't have access to.

    B. A GPF occurs when Windows attempts to write to an area of memory that it doesn't have access to.

    C. Windows will report the error occurrence, error location, and the application causing the error.

    D. A GPF can be caused by incompatible TSRs.

B, C, and D are the correct answers

CHAPTER 5

Navigating Windows 95 and Windows NT Workstation v4.0

INTRODUCTION TO MICROSOFT WINDOWS 95 AND NT V4.0

For review of this topic refer to Chapter 1.

Question ID: 12

Which of the following Windows products are 32-bit operating systems?

    A.   Windows v3.1

    B.   Windows for Workgroups v3.11

    C.   Windows 95

    D.   Windows NT Workstation v4.0

    E.   All of the Above

C and D are the correct answers

Question ID: 13

Which of the following features are supported by Windows 95, but not by Windows NT Workstation v4.0?

    A.   Plug and Play Technology

    B.   Preemptive Multitasking

    C.   Support for MS-DOS Device Drivers

    D.   RISC Processor Support

    E.   Support for Windows 16-bit Applications

A and C are the correct answers

Question ID: 14

Which of the following features are supported by Windows NT Workstation v4.0, but not by Windows 95?

    A.   Support for 32-bit Applications

    B.   Support for Roving Users

    C.   NTFS File System and Automatic Failure Recovery

    D.   Scaleable Multiprocessor Support Configurations

C and D are the correct answers

Question ID: 16

Which operating systems support the New Technology File System?

    A. Windows 95
    B. Windows v3.1
    C. DOS
    D. Windows NT
    E. OS/2

D is the correct answer

Question ID: 17

What does a partition contain when it is formatted with the FAT file system?

    A. BIOS Parameter Block with Boot Information
    B. Two copies of the File Allocation Table
    C. A Root Directory
    D. The File Area
    E. An Automatic Backup Cluster

A, B, C, and D are the correct answers

Question ID: 18

What are the advantages of the NTFS over the FAT file system?

    A. NTFS supports large files more optimally.
    B. NTFS contains a fully recoverable directory structure.
    C. NTFS supports rights assignments and auditing on a per-file basis.
    D. NTFS supports a partition size of 4 GB and FAT does not.
    E. NTFS can be used by both Windows NT and Windows 95 systems and FAT cannot.

A, B, and C are the correct answers

Question ID: 19

Select the NTFS file responsible for providing a recoverable file system.

    A. Log File ($LogFile)
    B. Master File Table ($Mft)
    C. Root Directory ($)
    D. Boot File ($Boot)
    E. All of the above

A is the correct answer

Question ID: 21

You need to make a decision on the standard operating system to be used at your enterprise. Your requirements include support for Win16 and Win32 applications, as well as file-level security for sensitive data files. Which Windows-family product would be the most appropriate choice?

    A. Windows v3.1
    B. Windows for Workgroups v3.11
    C. Windows 95
    D. Windows NT Workstation v4.0

D is the correct answer

Question ID: 22

Which of the following are features of both the Windows 95 and NT Workstation v4.0 user interface?

    A. The Task Bar
    B. The Windows Explorer
    C. The Program Manager
    D. Shortcuts
    E. Property Sheets

A, B, D, and E are the correct answers

Question ID: 34

What feature of Windows 95 replaces Windows v3.x 's feature of minimizing inactive applications?

A. Program Manager
B. Task Bar
C. Drag and Drop
D. Windows Explorer
E. Device Manager

B is the correct answer

Question ID: 129

Which of the following IS NOT an advantage of Windows NT over Windows 95?

A. Support for MIPS-, Alpha-, and PowerPC-based systems.
B. Plug and Play hardware support.
C. Support for multiprocessor configurations.
D. Preemptive multitasking for Win16-based applications.
E. All of the above are Windows NT advantages.

B is the correct answer

Question ID: 170

A customer asks you for a recommendation in regards to which operating system they should purchase. Their requirements include support for 32-bit Windows applications, a high degree of security, and RISC processor support. Which Windows-family member would meet these requirements?

A. Windows v3.x
B. Windows for Workgroups v3.1x
C. Windows 95
D. Windows NT Workstation v4.0
E. None of the listed Windows platforms will meet all stated requirements.

D is the correct answer

Question ID: 171

A customer asks you for a recommendation in regards to which operating system that they should purchase. Their requirements include support for MS-DOS based device drivers, full Plug and Play support, and RISC processor support. Which Windows-family member would meet these requirements?

A. Windows v3.x
B. Windows for Workgroups v3.1x
C. Windows 95
D. Windows NT Workstation v4.0
E. None of the listed Windows platforms will meet all stated requirements.

E is the correct answer

Question ID: 172

A customer asks you for a recommendation in regards to which operating system that they should purchase for their mobile systems. Their requirements include support for 32-bit and 16-bit Windows applications and MS-DOS device drivers. In addition, they require an operating system that provides full Plug and Play support. Which Windows-family member would meet these requirements?

A. Windows v3.x
B. Windows for Workgroups v3.1x
C. Windows 95
D. Windows NT Workstation v4.0
E. None of the listed Windows platforms will meet all stated requirements.

C is the correct answer

Question ID: 173

Select the true statements from those listed below.

A. The FAT file system does not support long filenames.
B. The maximum length of a file name under the FAT file system is 11 characters, including the extension.
C. Both NTFS and FAT use clusters to allocate files.
D. You can format a floppy diskette using the NTFS file system.
E. The maximum size of a file on a FAT file system is 2 GB.

C is the correct answer

Question ID: 192

You have a customer who has recently purchased Windows NT Workstation v4.0. They ask you for advice on the type of file system to utilize: FAT or NTFS. Which questions would be most pertinent to ask the customer to help determine the appropriate choice?

A. Do you need to dual boot with another operating system such as Windows 95?
B. Do you need support for 16-bit Windows applications?
C. Are you installing Windows NT on a RISC-based system?
D. Is security an overwhelming concern?
E. Will the computer be participating on a network?

A, C, and D are the correct answers

Question ID: 221

Win32 applications use _____ multitasking.

A. Single source
B. Cooperative
C. Elective
D. Preemptive
E. Variable

D is the correct answer

Question ID: 241

Which of the following statements are true?

A. The Windows 95 operating system must be installed on a FAT partition.
B. Windows 95 cannot install on an NTFS or HPFS partition, but after installation, a Windows 95 workstation can read information on NTFS or HPFS partitions.
C. Windows 95 can be installed on an NTFS (Windows NT) file partition or a FAT partition.
D. Windows 95 cannot be installed on an HPFS (OS/2) file partition.
E. Windows 95 can be installed on an NTFS, HPFS, or FAT partition.

A and D are the correct answers

Question ID: 245

Which of the following file systems support Windows 95 installation?

A. FAT
B. HPFS
C. NTFS
D. NFS
E. NVFS

A is the correct answer

Question ID: 258

Assuming your systems meet all other minimum requirements for installation, which of the following situations would cause a Windows 95 installation to fail?

A. The computer does not have an HPFS (OS/2) partition.
B. The hard disk does not have a file allocation table (FAT) partition.
C. The hard disk does not have an NTFS partition.
D. The hard disk does not have both an NTFS and an FAT partition.
E. None of the above would cause a Windows 95 installation to fail.

B is the correct answer

Question ID: 259

Michael and Bob are planning to expand their accounting firm. There will be about 40 employees added to the present staff. They want to implement a networking system which would allow them to run their old MS-DOS applications, which has preemptive multitasking capability, and which supports multiple threads of execution for 32-bit applications. They also need an integrated network system offering C2 level security. Which Windows-family member should they choose?

A. Windows NT Workstation v4.0
B. Windows v3.1
C. Windows 95
D. Windows for Workgroups v3.11
E. Any of the above operating systems will fulfill the above requirements.

A is the correct answer

Question ID: 287

Full preemptive multitasking is supported on which of the following platforms?

A. Windows NT v4.0 Workstation
B. Windows v3.1
C. Windows for Workgroups v3.11
D. MS-DOS v6.22
E. None of the above

A is the correct answer

Question ID: 331

As a new network administrator, you have been assigned to install client machines on the company's local network. You have to choose a platform that will provide 32-bit code support, meet C2 security specifications, and that will also support a wide variety of 16-bit Windows and MS-DOS applications in addition to native applications. Which of the following Windows-family members would meet your requirements?

    A.   Windows v3.1

    B.   Windows for Workgroups v3.11

    C.   Windows 95

    D.   Windows NT Workstation v4.0

D is the correct answer

Question ID: 380

Choose three features of the FAT32 file system.

    A.   FAT32 uses disk space more efficiently than FAT.

    B.   FAT32 is an enhanced version of the FAT file system.

    C.   FAT32 provides C2-level security.

    D.   FAT32 uses a smaller cluster size than FAT.

A, B, and D are the correct answers

Question ID: 381

Which of the following are included with the OSR2 version of Windows 95?

    A.   NetMeeting

    B.   FAT32

    C.   NTFS support

    D.   Infrared device drivers

A, B, and D are the correct answers

INSTALLING WINDOWS 95

For review of this topic refer to Chapter 2.

Question ID: 23

Which of the following are MINIMUM hardware requirements for running Windows 95?

A. 16 MB of memory

B. 80386SX Processor or higher

C. VGA Compatible Video Adapter

D. CD-ROM

E. 250 MB of hard drive space

B and C are the correct answers

Question ID: 25

What information do you have to provide during setup when upgrading a networked PC to Windows 95?

A. Default Username

B. Sound Card Settings

C. Computer Name

D. Workgroup Name

E. Network Password

A, C, and D are the correct answers

Question ID: 26

A salesman in your office uses a laptop for nearly all of his computing, which includes a lot of dial-up data transfer. You need to install Windows 95 on his system. Which installation method would you most likely select?

A. Typical
B. Compact
C. Portable
D. Custom
E. Laptop

C is the correct answer

Question ID: 28

Which of the following files are usually not required in order to boot the system under Windows 95?

A. COMMAND.COM
B. AUTOEXEC.BAT
C. IO.SYS
D. CONFIG.SYS
E. All of the above files are required.

B and D are the correct answers

Question ID: 29

Which of the following elements are configured when you start up Windows 95 for the first time?

A. Start Menu
B. Printers
C. Sound Card
D. Time Zone Information
E. None of the above

A, B, and D are the correct answers

Question ID: 30

Which of the following steps are part of the Windows 95 Setup process?

- A. Setup information and PC Hardware Detection
- B. Configuration Questions
- C. Copying Component Files
- D. Restart and Final Configuration
- E. All of the above

E is the correct answer

Question ID: 174

All of the following statements regarding Windows 95 installation are true EXCEPT:

- A. After installation, the original CONFIG.SYS and AUTOEXEC.BAT (if present) are renamed to CONFIG.DOS and AUTOEXEC.DOS.
- B. Minimum installation requirements for Windows 95 include a 80486SX or higher processor and 4 MB of RAM.
- C. Windows 95 can be installed across a network.
- D. The Windows 95 setup wizard provides four methods to complete an installation: Typical, Portable, Compact, or Custom.
- E. If you are upgrading from Windows v3.x, any existing program groups are converted to folders on the Start Menu.

B is the correct answer

Question ID: 242

The minimum operating system requirements for Windows 95 include:

   A.   MS-DOS v5.0 or higher, or an equivalent OEM version that supports disk partitions of 32 MB, Windows for Workgroups v3.1x, dual-boot MS-DOS with OS/2, or dual-boot MS-DOS with Windows NT.

   B.   MS-DOS 6.22 or higher, or an equivalent OEM version that supports disk partitions of 32 MB, Windows for Workgroups v3.1x, dual-boot MS-DOS with OS/2, or dual-boot MS-DOS with Windows NT.

   C.   Windows v3.1 and MS-DOS 6.x.

   D.   MS-DOS v3.2 or higher, or an equivalent OEM version that supports disk partitions of 32 MB, Windows for Workgroups v3.1x, dual-boot MS-DOS with OS/2, or dual-boot MS-DOS with Windows NT.

   E.   MS-DOS v3.2 or higher, or an equivalent OEM version that supports disk partitions of 32 MB, Windows for Workgroups v3.1x. Windows 95 will not install if Windows NT or OS/2 is present on the primary hard drive.

D is the correct answer

Question ID: 243

Windows 95 Setup supports four installation method selections. These are:

   A.   Typical, Portable, Compact, and Custom.

   B.   Typical, Mobile, Minimal, and Custom.

   C.   Typical, Laptop, Compact, and User-Defined.

   D.   Typical, Laptop, Minimal, and User-Defined.

   E.   Typical, Mobile, Compact, and User-Defined.

A is the correct answer

Question ID: 244

What is the minimum processor supported by Windows 95?

    A. 80286
    B. 80386SX
    C. 80386DX
    D. 80486SX
    E. 80486DX

C is the correct answer

Question ID: 246

When upgrading from Windows v3.x to Windows 95, what happens to existing Program Manager groups and items?

    A. They are lost.
    B. They are migrated to the Start menu.
    C. They are available only if you launch Program Manager after starting Windows 95.
    D. They are converted to desktop shortcuts.
    E. None of the above

B is the correct answer

Question ID: 247

Which of the following installation methods gives the greatest flexibility during installation?

    A. Typical
    B. Portable
    C. Compact
    D. Custom
    E. None of the above

D is the correct answer

Question ID: 248

Which of the following operating systems would support upgrade to Windows 95?

- A. MS-DOS 5.0
- B. MS-DOS 3.2
- C. Windows v3.1
- D. OS/2 v2.2
- E. OS/2 v3.0

A, B, and C are the correct answers

Question ID: 249

Which of the following statements can be said about Microsoft Network software?

- A. It is only installed on desktop systems.
- B. It is available as an option on all installations.
- C. It requires the Windows 95 Plus pack for installation.
- D. It requires TCP/IP for installation.
- E. None of the above

B is the correct answer

Question ID: 360

During installation, Windows 95 Setup creates four files that contain information about the setup and startup processes. What are the names of the four files?

- A. BOOTLOG.TXT, SETUPLOG.TXT, DETCRASH.LOG, and DETLOG.TXT
- B. BOOTLOG.LOG, SETUPLOG.LOG, DETCRASH.TXT, and DETLOG.TXT
- C. BOOTLOG.TXT, SETUPLOG.TXT, DETCRASH.TXT, and DETLOG.LOG
- D. BOOTLOG.LOG, SETUPLOG.LOG, DETCRASH.LOG, and DETLOG.TXT

A is the correct answer

Question ID: 361

Which of the following statements correctly describes the purpose of the BOOTLOG.TXT file?

A. This file contains information about the boot process. Problems that pertain to the startup of Windows 95 are recorded in this file.

B. This file contains information that allows Setup to recover if failure occurs before hardware detection.

C. This file contains information that allows Setup to recover if failure occurs during hardware detection.

D. This file is the equivalent of the DETCRASH.LOG but is created whether or not the installation is successful.

A is the correct answer

Question ID: 362

Which of the following statements correctly describes the purpose of the SETUPLOG.TXT file?

A. This file contains information about the boot process. Problems that pertain to the startup of Windows 95 are recorded in this file.

B. This file contains information that allows Setup to recover if failure occurs before hardware detection.

C. This file contains information that allows Setup to recover if failure occurs during hardware detection.

D. This file is the equivalent of the DETCRASH.LOG but is created whether or not the installation is successful.

B is the correct answer

Question ID: 363

Which of the following statements correctly describes the purpose of the DETCRASH.LOG file?

A. This file contains information about the boot process. Problems that pertain to the startup of Windows 95 are recorded in this file.
B. This file contains information that allows Setup to recover if failure occurs before hardware detection.
C. This file contains information that allows Setup to recover if failure occurs during hardware detection.
D. This file is the equivalent of the BOOTLOG.TXT but is created whether or not the installation is successful.

C is the correct answer

Question ID: 364

Which of the following statements correctly describes the purpose of the DETLOG.TXT file?

A. This file contains information about the boot process. Problems that pertain to the startup of Windows 95 are recorded in this file.
B. This file contains information that allows Setup to recover if failure occurs before hardware detection.
C. This file contains information that allows Setup to recover if failure occurs during hardware detection.
D. This file is the equivalent of the DETCRASH.LOG but is created whether or not the installation is successful.

D is the correct answer

Question ID: 386

Susan wants to have a choice between booting to MS-DOS/Windows 3.x or Windows 95. What statement should she place in the MSDOS.SYS file?

A. DualBoot=1
B. MultiBoot=1
C. MultiBoot=0
D. BootMulti=1

D is the correct answer

Question ID: 387

To enable a dual-boot configuration between MS-DOS/Windows 3.x and Windows 95, the BootMulti=1 statement should be placed in which file?

    A. CONFIG.SYS

    B. IO.SYS

    C. AUTOEXEC.BAT

    D. MSDOS.SYS

D is the correct answer

WINDOWS 95 BASICS

For review of this topic refer to Chapter 3.

Question ID: 15

What feature of Windows 95 replaces the File Manager?

A.   The Task Bar
B.   Windows Explorer
C.   The Start Menu
D.   The Desktop
E.   Device Manager

B is the correct answer

Question ID: 33

Which of the following are options when you select Shut Down from the Start menu?

A.   Shut down the computer?
B.   Restart the computer?
C.   Restart the computer in MS-DOS mode?
D.   Log on to the network?
E.   Close all programs and log on as a different user?

A, B, C, and E are the correct answers

Question ID: 36

What directory stores all items that you place on your Windows 95 desktop?

A.   C:\WINDOWS\SYSTEM
B.   C:\WINDOWS\DESKTOP
C.   C:\WINDOWS\SYSTEM\DESKTOP
D.   C:\WINDOWS
E.   C:\MY DOCUMENTS

B is the correct answer

Question ID: 37

You have received a call from Lisa, a Windows 95 user wanting to change her screen saver. Which of the following instructions would you give her to walk her through this procedure?

    A. Click on the secondary mouse button on the desktop, select Properties, then select the Screen Saver tab.

    B. Click on the primary mouse button on the desktop, select Properties, then select the Appearance tab.

    C. Click on the secondary mouse button on the desktop, then select the Screen Saver menu item.

    D. Click on the primary mouse button on the desktop, then select the Appearance menu item.

    E. Double-click on Control Panel and click on the Screen Saver icon using the secondary mouse button.

A is the correct answer

Question ID: 38

When you click the secondary mouse button on the desktop and select Properties, what features are you able to change in the Display Properties dialog box?

    A. Windows Color Schemes

    B. Wallpaper

    C. Mouse Settings

    D. Monitor Resolution

    E. Hard Drive Properties

A, B, and D are the correct answers

Question ID: 39

Paul has called and asked you to walk him through adding a program shortcut to his Windows 95 Start Menu. Which of the following procedures will you give Paul?

A. Click on the secondary mouse button on the desktop and select Create Shortcut.
B. Drag the program icon from its current location and drop it on the Start button.
C. Click on the Start menu and select Settings. Select the Task Bar item, then select the Start menu Options tab and click Add.
D. Click on the secondary mouse button on a blank area of the Task Bar. Select Properties, then select Add on the Start menu Options tab.
E. None of the above

B is the correct answer

Question ID: 40

What is the MS-DOS filename extension for Windows 95 shortcuts?

A. .SCT
B. .INI
C. .DLL
D. .EXE
E. .LNK

E is the correct answer

Question ID: 41

Select the items found under the My Computer icon in Windows 95.

A. Network Neighborhood
B. Control Panel
C. Recycle Bin
D. Dial-Up Networking
E. All Disk Drives

B, D, and E are the correct answers

Question ID: 42

Which of the following statements about the Windows 95 Control Panel are true?

    A. Control Panel objects can be moved and renamed.
    B. You can access the Control Panel by selecting RUN from the Start menu and typing CONTROL.
    C. Programs can be added and removed through the Control Panel.
    D. You can set the date and time through the Control Panel.
    E. You can shut down Windows 95 from within the Control Panel.

B, C, and D are the correct answers

Question ID: 43

Which of the following statements about the Windows 95 Recycle Bin are true?

    A. By default, 5% of your hard drive is reserved for the Recycle Bin.
    B. You can change the amount of hard drive space reserved for the Recycle Bin.
    C. Once the Recycle Bin is full, files are deleted on a first in/first out basis.
    D. Deleted items cannot be recovered.
    E. You must manually create the Recycle Bin; it is not created during setup.

B and C are the correct answers

Question ID: 177

By default, Windows 95 sets aside ___% of your total hard disk space for the Recycle Bin.

    A. 5
    B. 10
    C. 15
    D. 20

B is the correct answer

Question ID: 223

The Start menu contains the following items by default EXCEPT:

A. Network Neighborhood
B. Find
C. Programs
D. Documents
E. Shut Down

A is the correct answer

Question ID: 224

Which of the following statements about a shortcut are true?

A. It has properties.
B. It cannot be renamed.
C. It cannot be moved.
D. It can point to a network resource.
E. It has an MS-DOS filename estension of LNK.

A, D, and E are the correct answers

Question ID: 225

The Display property sheet allows you to:

A. Select wallpaper.
B. Change colors of desktop icons.
C. Change the Desktop size.
D. Create animated cursors.
E. Define a screen saver selection.

A, C, and E are the correct answers

Question ID: 226

What is the significance of the "Target" in a shortcut's properties?

    A. It is the physical location of the shortcut.

    B. It is the location of the object to which the shortcut points.

    C. It is the location of the shortcut's icon file.

    D. It is the location of the default working directory.

    E. None of the above

B is the correct answer

Question ID: 232

Which of the following statements about the Taskbar are true?

    A. Displays only minimized applications.

    B. Displays only maximized applications.

    C. Displays all running applications.

    D. Launches the selected applications.

    E. Contains the Start button.

C and E are the correct answers

Question ID: 233

Which of the following does NOT provide a way of accessing the contents of the Control Panel?

    A. Start Menu

    B. My Computer object

    C. Network Neighborhood object

    D. Explorer

    E. My Briefcase

C and E are the correct answers

Question ID: 234

The "My Computer" object:

    A. Is on the desktop by default.

    B. Cannot be renamed.

    C. Contains all resources available to the computer.

    D. Contains persistant network connections.

    E. Contains the Printers folder.

A, D, and E are the correct answers

Question ID: 235

The Recycle Bin:

    A. Allows you to set properties either globally or independently for each drive.

    B. Permanently deletes file on a last-in, first-out basis.

    C. Can be renamed by displaying its popup menu and running Rename.

    D. Is allocated reserved disk space as a percentage of total drive capacity.

    E. Allows you to salvage deleted files by dragging them out of the Recycle Bin to a folder or to the desktop.

A, D, and E are the correct answers

Question ID: 236

Which of the following is NOT a supported Explorer view?

    A. Text-only

    B. Small icon

    C. Large icon

    D. List

    E. Details

A is the correct answer

Question ID: 237

Which of the following are top-level Start menu selections?

    A. Programs--program menus
    B. Documents--recently opened documents
    C. Applications--recently launched applications
    D. Help--online help system
    E. Shut Down--shut down the system

A, B, D, and E are the correct answers

Question ID: 238

Which key combination calls the Start menu?

    A. <CTRL><ENTER>
    B. <CTRL><ESC>
    C. <ALT><ESC>
    D. <ALT><M>
    E. <ALT><F1>

B is the correct answer

Question ID: 239

What is the purpose of the Briefcase?

    A. It provides secure, password protected storage of files.
    B. It acts as an alternate Recycle Bin.
    C. It contains all archived Microsoft Mail messages.
    D. It provides file synchronization between two or more computers.
    E. None of the above

D is the correct answer

Question ID: 240

What happens when the Recycle Bin becomes full?

    A.   It will not accept any new files until emptied.

    B.   Files are permanently deleted on a first-in, first-out basis.

    C.   Its size is increased as needed "on the fly."

    D.   Any new files for the Recycle Bin are permanently deleted instead.

    E.   None of the above

B is the correct answer

Question ID: 250

How can you display a Desktop object's Property sheet?

    A.   Right-click on the object and press <P> on the keyboard.

    B.   Right-click on the object, and select Properties from the context-sensitive menu.

    C.   Left-click on an object, wait a moment, and left-click again.

    D.   Double-click on an object.

    E.   Select an object and press <F1>.

B is the correct answer

Question ID: 365

Which of the following statements accurately describe features of Windows 95 printing?

    A.   Ease of printer setup and support because of improvements in the UI and Plug and Play support

    B.   Better performance with the use of an improved 16-bit printing architecture

    C.   Better integration of network printing through extension of the Windows 95 printing architecture to the network environment

    D.   Quicker "return-to-application" time because of the use of Enhanced MetaFile (EMF) spooling

A, C, and D are the correct answers

Question ID: 366

Which of the following are valid paths to the Printers folder?

    A. Start/Settings/Printers

    B. Start/Settings/Control Panel/Printers

    C. My Computer/Printers

    D. Start/Programs/Accessories/System Tools/Printers

A, B, and C are the correct answers

Question ID: 367

Joseph has purchased a new printer and has asked for your help. Which of the following methods could Joseph use to install the printer on his Windows 95 computer?

    A. During Setup, when prompted to add a printer

    B. After Setup, using the Control Panel System utility

    C. Automatically, using a Plug and Play printer

    D. Using Point and Print

A, C, and D are the correct answers

Question ID: 368

Of the following four statements, please select the ones that accurately describe features of Windows 95 print queue management.

    A. To reorder a print job waiting in the queue, drag it to the desired position.

    B. Current print jobs cannot be reordered; they can only be deleted.

    C. Current print jobs cannot be deleted.

    D. Jobs in the print queue cannot be reordered.

A and B are the correct answers

Question ID: 384

Which of the following statements are true?

A. Deferred printing allows the user to queue print jobs to a defined network printer that is not physically connected to the network.

B. Deferred printing holds the print job on a network server until the printer becomes available.

C. With deferred printing, the print job remains in the queue until the printer becomes available.

D. Deferred printing cannot be used on mobile computers.

A and C are the correct answers

Question ID: 385

Which of the following statements are true?

A. Certain applications can only print to drivers that generate raw printer data.

B. Spooling refers to the temporary storage of print jobs on the hard drive.

C. Windows 95 spools raw printer data to the hard drive as it prepares to print.

D. Windows 3.1 spools raw printer data to the hard drive as it prepares to print.

A, B, and D are the correct answers

WINDOWS 95 HARDWARE MANAGEMENT

For review of this topic refer to Chapter 4.

Question ID: 44

You have recommended to your manager that all new workstations use the Windows 95 platform, as opposed to Windows NT Workstation, because of its Plug and Play support. When you are asked to explain the benefits of Plug and Play, which of the following would be appropriate?

A. Full compatibility and support for legacy hardware.

B. Support for mobile computing.

C. Automated configuration and installation of Plug and Play peripherals.

D. Centralized hardware configuration information in the Windows 95 Registry.

E. All of the above are benefits derived from Windows 95's Plug and Play support.

E is the correct answer

Question ID: 45

Select the Windows 95 component that stores hardware and software configuration information.

A. Control Panel

B. HKEY_LOCAL_MACHINE

C. The Registry

D. .INI Files

E. My Computer

C is the correct answer

Question ID: 46

What sub-tree of the Windows 95 Registry stores all hardware configuration information?

    A. HKEY_LOCAL_MACHINE
    B. HKEY_CURRENT_USER
    C. HKEY_CLASSES_ROOT
    D. REGEDIT.EXE
    E. HKEY_LOCAL_DEVICES

A is the correct answer

Question ID: 47

Which of the following components are found in the Windows 95 System object?

    A. Device Manager
    B. Performance
    C. Network Neighborhood
    D. Multimedia
    E. Hardware Profiles

A, B, and E are the correct answers

Question ID: 48

You are dispatched to a Windows 95 workstation. The modem is not working. When you access the Device Manager, you notice that the modem that has an icon of a circled exclamation point next to it. What does this mean?

    A. The modem is configured properly.
    B. The modem is functioning properly.
    C. The modem has a device conflict.
    D. A modem is not installed.
    E. The modem has been disabled.

C is the correct answer

Question ID: 49

Which of the following computer properties can you view through the Windows 95 Device Manager?

    A. IRQ Settings
    B. DMA Settings
    C. Percentages of Available Resources
    D. I/O Settings
    E. Memory Requirements

A, B, and D are the correct answers

Question ID: 50

You are assigned to configuring all of the Windows 95 laptops that your company's sales force uses. The salespeople will use the laptops for dial-up networking, at a docking station on-site, and sometimes without a network connection. What would you do to allow salespeople to easily use their laptops in these different situations?

    A. Create a batch file to handle these different situations.
    B. Set up different hardware profiles through the System property sheet.
    C. Provide laptops for off-site work and desktop PC's for on-site connectivity.
    D. Install Windows NT on the laptops.
    E. None of the above

B is the correct answer

Question ID: 52

Which of the following statements about virtual memory management under Windows 95 are true?

    A. Swap files change sizes dynamically.
    B. Swap files can be located on a fragmented portion of the hard drive.
    C. Virtual memory algorithms and access methods have been improved.
    D. Swap files require contiguous disk space and cannot be used on drives that are fragmented.
    E. Windows 95 swap files operate identically to those used in Windows v3.1.

A, B, and C are the correct answers

Question ID: 53

You have just installed a new sound card in your system and determine that it has a conflict with another device. What resource can help you resolve this conflict?

    A.   Memory Troubleshooter in Windows Help

    B.   Registry

    C.   Hardware Conflict Troubleshooter in Windows Help

    D.   System Performance property sheet

    E.   Control Panel

C is the correct answer

Question ID: 54

Under which of the following situations would you access Windows 95's Safe Mode?

    A.   Windows 95 does not boot up properly.

    B.   You receive an "out of memory" error in Microsoft Excel.

    C.   You want to recover the contents of the Recycle Bin.

    D.   You are using a laptop computer.

    E.   You need extra virus protection.

A is the correct answer

Question ID: 109

Select the utility that is used to change Registry information.

    A.   Regulator

    B.   Regedit

    C.   Sysreg

    D.   Regmod

    E.   Sysedit

B is the correct answer

Question ID: 179

The Windows 95 Startup Menu provides all of the following options EXCEPT:

    A. Normal
    B. Safe Mode
    C. Safe Mode with Network Support
    D. Normal Mode with Network Support
    E. Safe Mode Command Prompt Only

D is the correct answer

Question ID: 181

A customer calls with a problem they are having with their network adapter. Upon investigation, you find a red "X" over the Network Adapter icon in the Device Manager. What does this most likely indicate?

    A. The device is causing a hardware conflict.
    B. The device is failing due to incorrect drivers.
    C. The device is disabled in the current hardware profile.
    D. The device is failing due to a hardware malfunction.

C is the correct answer

Question ID: 183

The Plug and Play architecture consists of all of the following components EXCEPT:

    A. Plug and Play Hardware Devices
    B. Plug and Play Software Drivers
    C. Plug and Play Operating System
    D. Plug and Play BIOS

B is the correct answer

Question ID: 184

Under Windows 95, the _____ sub-tree in the Registry Editor stores all hardware configuration information.

    A. HKEY_CLASSES_ROOT
    B. HKEY_CURRENT_USER
    C. HKEY_LOCAL_MACHINE
    D. HKEY_USERS
    E. HKEY_HARDWARE_CONFIG

C is the correct answer

Question ID: 185

Which of the following statements are false?

    A. Windows 95 virtual memory uses a permanent swap file.
    B. Windows 95 virtual memory uses a temporary swap file.
    C. Under Windows 95, you can place the swap file on a compressed drive.
    D. A fragmented hard disk causes the operating system to search a larger physical area of the disk in order to find information.
    E. Under Windows 95, ScanDisk provides disk defragmentation services.

A and E are the correct answers

Question ID: 222

The Plug and Play architecture consists of the following components EXCEPT:

    A. Plug and Play software
    B. Plug and Play BIOS
    C. Plug and Play hardware devices
    D. Plug and Play operating systems
    E. None of the above

A is the correct answer

Question ID: 229

While using the Device Manager utility, you notice a device listed with an exclamation point. Which of the following best describes the problem state?

A. The device is disabled, but is physically present and is consuming resources; it does not have a Windows 95 driver loaded.

B. The device is disabled because it has been removed from the system and Windows 95 did not load the driver.

C. The device is in a problem state because Windows 95 tried to load a driver, but failed.

D. Windows 95 had to load a protected mode driver instead of the appropriate real-mode driver.

C is the correct answer

Question ID: 230

Which of the following statements about the Device Manager are true?

A. It is launched as a unique Control Panel object.

B. It is accessed through the Device Manager tab under the System Control Panel object

C. It is accessed through the Device Manager tab under the Add New Hardware Control Panel object.

D. It is only available when you are in Safe Mode.

E. None of the above

B is the correct answer

Question ID: 251

Which of the following statements about the Device Manager are correct?

A. It provides the user with graphical indications of hardware problems.

B. It supports Drag and Drop installation of new Plug and Play devices.

C. It allows the user to change resource settings for devices.

D. It displays all devices attached to the computer in a graphical manner.

E. It allows the user to start the Add New Hardware wizard by clicking on the New button.

A, C, and D are the correct answers

Question ID: 252

Which of the following statements about Windows 95 device support are true?

A. Support is provided for Plug and Play devices.
B. Support is provided for legacy devices.
C. Hot swapping is not supported.
D. Hardware configuration is stored in the HARDWARE.INI file.
E. Windows 95 configures Plug and Play devices automatically.

A, B, and E are the correct answers

Question ID: 253

How are disabled devices identified under the Device Manager?

A. The device entry cannot be opened.
B. There is a red "X" through the device icon.
C. There is a black exclamation mark in a yellow circle over the device icon.
D. There is a red question mark over the device icon.
E. None of the above

B is the correct answer

Question ID: 254

Which of the following statements are true about Windows 95 Safe Mode?

A. A minimal set of device drivers, including VGA video and Microsoft Mouse drivers, are loaded.
B. You can force a system into Safe Mode by pressing <F8> after restarting when "Starting Windows 95..." appears on the screen.
C. You can launch Windows 95 in the Safe Mode by restarting in MS-DOS mode and typing "WIN /SAFE" at the command prompt.
D. Safe Mode includes support for PCMCIA and CD-ROM devices.
E. It is a special diagnostic mode of Windows that allows you to fix problems that keep you from starting Windows 95 properly.

A, B, and E are the correct answers

Question ID: 255

Which of the following are NOT supported under Safe Mode?

    A. CD-ROM

    B. VGA resolution

    C. Hard disk

    D. Mouse

    E. PCMCIA devices

A and E are the correct answers

Question ID: 256

You suspect hard disk media errors. Which of the following Windows 95 utilities should you run to verify this?

    A. ChkDisk

    B. ScanDisk

    C. DeFrag

    D. DiskDiag

    E. DriveSpc

B is the correct answer

Question ID: 262

Which of the following Windows 95 utilities can be used to optimize the performance of your hard disk?

    A. FDISK

    B. DriveSpace

    C. Disk Defragmenter

    D. Scan Disk

    E. Disk Optimizer

C is the correct answer

Question ID: 264

While using the Device Manager utility, you notice a device listed with an exclamation point. Which of the following best describes the problem state?

A.   The device is disabled, but is physically present and is consuming resources but does not have a Windows 95 driver loaded.

B.   The device is disabled because it has been removed from the system and Windows 95 did not load the driver.

C.   The device is in a problem state because Windows 95 tried to load a driver, but failed.

D.   Windows 95 had to load a protected mode driver instead of the appropriate real-mode driver.

C is the correct answer

Question ID: 369

You are currently using Microsoft Backup for Windows 95. What are the two types of backups available with this program?

A.   Daily

B.   Partial

C.   Incremental

D.   Full

C and D are the correct answers

Question ID: 370

Which of the following statements accurately describe the VFAT?

A.   The 32-bit Virtual File Allocation Table is the primary file system.

B.   VFAT uses only protected-mode drivers.

C.   The structure of FAT on the disk remains the same as in previous versions.

D.   VFAT uses 16-bit code to handle all file access.

A and C are the correct answers

Question ID: 371

Which of the following statements accurately describe the CDFS?

    A. The Virtual CDFS (VCDFS) handles information on CD-ROMs just as VFAT handles information on a hard disk.

    B. The CDFS driver loads dynamically upon detection of an attached CD-ROM.

    C. CDFS is a protected-mode version of MSCDEX.EXE.

    D. CDFS is a real-mode version of MSCDEX.EXE.

A, B, and C are the correct answers

WINDOWS 95 SOFTWARE MANAGEMENT

For review of this topic refer to Chapter 5.

Question ID: 55

Which of the following types of applications are supported by Windows 95?

    A. DOS-based Programs

    B. UNIX-based Programs

    C. 16-bit Windows Programs

    D. 32-bit Windows Programs

    E. Macintosh Programs

A, C, and D are the correct answers

Question ID: 56

What is the term for the technique where 16-bit code calls 32-bit codes and vice-versa?

    A. Virtual Memory

    B. Chunking

    C. Virtual Machine

    D. DLL

    E. Thunking

E is the correct answer

Question ID: 57

Where do 16-bit Windows applications reside under Windows 95?

    A. DOS Virtual Machine

    B. Individual Address Space in the System Virtual Machine

    C. Shared Memory Address Space in the System Virtual Machine

    D. Shared Memory Address Space in the DOS Virtual Machine

    E. None of the above

C is the correct answer

Question ID: 58

Which of the following elements are contained in a virtual machine?

    A. Virtual Address Space in Physical or Virtual Memory

    B. Processor Registers

    C. Privileges

    D. Hardware Profiles

    E. All of the above

A, B, and C are the correct answers

Question ID: 59

What interface provides support for MS-DOS, 16-bit and 32-bit applications under Windows 95?

    A. Win32API

    B. GUI

    C. Win16API

    D. USER.EXE

    E. VER.DLL

A is the correct answer

Question ID: 60

Which of the following statements are true regarding DOS programs running under Windows 95 as compared to Windows 3.x?

    A. MS-DOS programs run full-screen by default.

    B. MS-DOS programs are set to run in background mode by default.

    C. MS-DOS programs can be allocated 100% of system resources.

    D. When running under Windows 95, much more conventional memory is available to MS-DOS applications.

    E. All of the above

B, C, and D are the correct answers

Question ID: 61

Which of the following 32-bit protected mode drivers replace 16-bit drivers, allowing more conventional memory for MS-DOS applications under Windows 95?

    A. SHARE.EXE

    B. HIMEM.SYS

    C. EMM386.EXE

    D. MOUSE.COM

    E. SMARTDRV.EXE

A, D, and E are the correct answers

Question ID: 62

Which of the following activities CANNOT be accomplished from the Add/Remove Programs object in the Windows 95 Control Panel?

    A. Create a Windows 95 startup disk.

    B. Add the Microsoft Exchange component.

    C. Uninstall an application.

    D. Install a new printer.

    E. Modify sounds associated with system events.

D and E are the correct answers

Question ID: 63

What will happen when a 16-bit Windows application violates system integrity in Windows 95?

    A. All open MS-DOS, 16-bit, and 32-bit applications will lock up.

    B. All open 16-bit applications will lock up.

    C. Only the application that violates system integrity will lock up.

    D. The entire system will lock up.

    E. Windows 95 will continue to function normally and no applications will lock.

B is the correct answer

Question ID: 64

What will happen when a 32-bit Windows application fails to respond to messages sent to it from the Windows 95 operating system?

   A. All open MS-DOS, 16-bit, and 32-bit applications will lock up.
   B. All open 32-bit applications will lock up.
   C. Only the application that violates system integrity will lock up.
   D. The entire system will lock up.
   E. Nothing out of the ordinary will happen.

C is the correct answer

Question ID: 66

You receive a call from Jennifer. Microsoft Word has locked up on her Windows 95 workstation. She tells you that she also has Excel open and hasn't had an opportunity to save a spreadsheet she is working on. Select the procedure below that you would pass along to Jennifer.

   A. Minimize the Word program and give it an opportunity to fix itself.
   B. Power down the system.
   C. Press <CTRL><ALT><DEL> until the system reboots.
   D. Press <ESC> to terminate the program.
   E. Press <CTRL><ALT><DEL>, select the Word program and click on End Task.

A are the correct answers

Question ID: 67

You are in a DOS session under Windows 95. How can you quickly view the document README.TXT from the DOS prompt?

   A. Type README.TXT at the command prompt.
   B. Type VIEW README.TXT at the command prompt.
   C. Type START README.TXT at the command prompt.
   D. Type README.TXT START at the command prompt.
   E. Type SHOW README.TXT at the command prompt.

C is the correct answer

Question ID: 68

Where are the new DOS commands stored under a Windows 95 environment?

A. C:\DOS
B. C:\WINDOWS\COMMAND
C. C:\DOS\COMMAND
D. C:\WINDOWS\DOS
E. C:\WINDOWS\SYSTEM\DOS

B is the correct answer

Question ID: 186

In Windows 95, the System Virtual Machine contains:

A. Base system components, such as GDI, USER, and Kernel.
B. Shared memory address space shared by all Windows 16-bit applications.
C. Shared memory address space shared by all Windows 32-bit applications.
D. Shared memory address space shared by all MS-DOS applications.
E. Individual memory address spaces for each Windows 16-bit application.

A and B are the correct answers

Question ID: 188

A customer calls with a problem. They have a Windows application that frequently locks up. When this occurs, all other applications that are currently open lock up as well, except for one newer word processing application. Given this information, which of the below statements are true?

A. The application that is locking up is most likely a 16-bit application.
B. The application that is locking up is most likely a 32-bit application.
C. The application that does NOT lock up is most likely a 16-bit application.
D. The application that does NOT lock up is most likely a 32-bit application.
E. The application that does NOT lock up must be an MS-DOS based application.

A and D are the correct answers

Question ID: 189

At the Windows 95 command prompt, you type START PAINT.EXE /m. What does this command accomplish?

    A. PAINT.EXE will start up in a maximized state (in the foreground).

    B. PAINT.EXE will start up in a minimized state (in the background).

    C. PAINT.EXE will start up and ask you to load a file.

    D. The system returns an error message.

B is the correct answer

Question ID: 227

Which of the following will run in a shared address space?

    A. MS-DOS applications

    B. Win16 applications

    C. Win32 applications

    D. POSIX applications

    E. None of the above

B is the correct answer

Question ID: 228

Which of the following will each run in a separate virtual machine?

    A. MS-DOS applications

    B. Win16 (Windows v3.x) applications

    C. Win 32 applications

    D. POSIX applications

    E. None of the above

A is the correct answer

Question ID: 257

What key combination do you press in Windows 95 to display all active applications so you can select and manually terminate a locked application?

    A.   <CTRL><ESC>

    B.   <ALT><ESC>

    C.   <CTRL><ALT><DEL>

    D.   <SHIFT><F8>

    E.   None of the above

C is the correct answer

Question ID: 260

You have recently upgraded your system from Windows v3.1 to Windows 95. Sometimes when you run your 16-bit applications, one of them has a problem and other Win16-based applications then fail also. Every time this happens you have to do a local reboot to get your system up and running. Why aren't the 16-bit applications protected?

    A.   There may be a virus in one of the affected applications.

    B.   There is something wrong with one of the applications forcing it to write to all other application's memory areas and causing other applications to fail when it does.

    C.   One of the MS-DOS applications may have a problem, which is causing all Win16-based applications to fail.

    D.   All Win16-based applications share memory space and application queues, so one malfunctioning Win16-based application causes other Win16-based applications to fail.

D is the correct answer

Question ID: 263

You have an MS-DOS game that cannot be configured to run under Windows 95. What do you need to configure in order to run the DOS-based game?

A. Use the PIF editor to allow the game to run full-screen.

B. Alternate click the game icon, select Run Full-screen.

C. Alternate click the game icon, select Properties, select Program, select Advanced and configure the game to run maximized.

D. Alternate click the game icon, select Properties, select Program, select Advanced and configure the game to run in MS-DOS mode.

D is the correct answer

BASIC MANAGEMENT

For review of this topic refer to Chapter 6.

Question ID: 31

You are a network administrator and need to set user access controls to Windows 95. What utility allows you to set these parameters?

A. CONTROL
B. POLEDIT
C. PASSWORD
D. ACCESS
E. WINFILE

B is the correct answer

Question ID: 69

Select the files that make up the Windows 95 Registry.

A. USER.DAT
B. REGISTER.DAT
C. REGEDIT.EXE
D. SYSTEM.DAT
E. PROFILE.DAT

A and D are the correct answers

Question ID: 70

What are the advantages of storing Windows 95 Registry information in two different files?

    A. Components can be located in different areas on a network and a local hard drive to give the system administrator flexibility.

    B. Multiple users can share the same PC while maintaining their specific configurations.

    C. Virtual memory is optimized.

    D. Allowing a PC to store Registry files on a file server provides support for diskless workstations

    E. System resources are used more efficiently.

A, B, and D are the correct answers

Question ID: 71

Select the features of Windows 95 Dial-Up Networking.

    A. Advanced Security and Modem Support

    B. Automatic Compression

    C. Support for Microsoft RAS

    D. Support for the PPP Protocol

    E. All of the above

E is the correct answer

Question ID: 372

Windows 95 recommends that you create a Startup disk during installation. How do you create a Startup disk after Windows 95 has been installed?

    A. With the System Tools utility

    B. With the Control Panel System utility

    C. With the Windows 95 Explorer

    D. Control Panel Add/Remove Programs utility

D is the correct answer

Question ID: 373

The Connection tab of the Modems Properties sheet provides a checkbox that can be selected to record a modem error log file for troubleshooting purposes. What is the name of the file that is recorded and where is it located?

A. C:\ERRORLOG.TXT

B. C:\MODEMLOG.LOG

C. C:\WINDOWS\ERRORLOG.TXT

D. C:\WINDOWS\MODEMLOG.TXT

D is the correct answer

Question ID: 374

Karen is receiving a "Bad or Missing Command Interpreter" error on her Windows 95 workstation. What could be the problem?

A. IFSHLP.SYS file is missing from the Windows folder.

B. COMMAND.COM is missing the IFSHLP.SYS statement.

C. CONFIG.SYS is missing the IFSHLP.SYS statement.

D. The COMMAND.COM file is corrupted or missing.

D is the correct answer

Question ID: 375

Tim calls and reports that he has a VFAT initialization error. Select the possible cause(s) of this error.

A. IFSHLP.SYS file is missing from the Windows folder.

B. COMMAND.COM is missing the IFSHLP.SYS statement.

C. CONFIG.SYS is missing the IFSHLP.SYS statement.

D. The COMMAND.COM file is corrupted or missing.

A and C are the correct answers

Question ID: 376

Which of the following file system troubleshooting options should be selected when an MS-DOS application is experiencing problems with sharing (SHARE.EXE) in Windows 95?

    A. Disable new file sharing and locking semantics.
    B. Disable long filename preservation for old programs.
    C. Disable all 32-bit protect-mode disk drivers.
    D. Disable write-behind caching for all drives.

A is the correct answer

Question ID: 377

Your office is using a legacy application that does not provide support for long filenames. Which of the following file system troubleshooting options should you select?

    A. Disable new file sharing and locking semantics.
    B. Disable long filename preservation for old programs.
    C. Disable all 32-bit protect-mode disk drivers.
    D. Disable write-behind caching for all drives.

B is the correct answer

Question ID: 378

Which of the following file system troubleshooting options should be selected if you are having problems with a hard drive that is not fully compatible with Windows 95?

    A. Disable new file sharing and locking semantics.
    B. Disable long filename preservation for old programs.
    C. Disable all 32-bit protect-mode disk drivers.
    D. Disable write-behind caching for all drives.

C is the correct answer

Question ID: 379

Which of the following file system troubleshooting options should be selected if you want caching to be enabled for read activities only?

    A. Disable new file sharing and locking semantics.
    B. Disable long filename preservation for old programs.
    C. Disable all 32-bit protect-mode disk drivers.
    D. Disable write-behind caching for all drives.

D is the correct answer

Question ID: 382

Which of the following statements are true?

    A. You cannot perform bi-directional printing with a uni-directional cable.
    B. You can perform bi-directional printing with a uni-directional cable.
    C. Printing problems can be caused by problems with the hard disk.
    D. Running a disk defragmentation program may solve some printing problems.

A, C, and D are the correct answers

Question ID: 383

You have created a Windows 95 Startup disk. Which of the following files would you find on this disk?

    A. REGEDIT.EXE
    B. UNINSTAL.EXE
    C. SETVER.EXE
    D. EDIT.COM

A, B, and D are the correct answers

INSTALLING WINDOWS NT WORKSTATION V4.0

For review of this topic refer to Chapter 7.

Question ID: 80

Your co-worker is installing Windows NT Workstation on his computer. He is considering using the FAT system as opposed to NTFS. You caution him that, depending on his circumstances, he may want reconsider his decision. Which of the following are situations where NTFS should be used?

    A. If security is an overwhelming concern, he should use NTFS.

    B. If he doesn't want to allow local access after booting from another operating system, he should use NTFS.

    C. If he wants to be able to use FAT utilities.

    D. If his workstation is a RISC-based system, he'll need to use NTFS.

    E. All of the above are reasons for using NTFS.

A and B are the correct answers

Question ID: 81

Your company has decided to use Windows NT Workstation as the operating system for all new workstations. It is your responsibility to determine the standard workstation configuration to be used. You are debating if you should recommend the FAT file system over NTFS. Select the circumstances where FAT is required.

    A. If you want dual-boot capabilities, you must use FAT.

    B. If you do not want to allow local access after booting from another operating system, you should use FAT.

    C. If you want to be able to use DOS-based file utilities, you must use FAT.

    D. If you are installing Windows NT Workstation on RISC-based systems, you must use FAT.

    E. All of the above are situations where the FAT file system is required.

A, C, and D are the correct answers

Question ID: 82

Which of the following Windows NT Workstation installation methods provides the best alternate support for Proprietary HALs, system timing, and third-party device drivers?

A. Network Installation

B. WINNT.EXE

C. Boot Installation

D. SETUPLDR

E. Custom Installation

C is the correct answer

Question ID: 83

What do we call the component of Windows NT Workstation that interfaces the operating system to the computer hardware?

A. Plug and Play

B. Hardware Profiles

C. Device Manager

D. NTFS

E. Hardware Abstraction Layer

E is the correct answer

Question ID: 84

Which of the following HALs are shipped with Windows NT Workstation v4.0?

A. HALs for Intel-based PCs

B. HALs for MIPS

C. HALs for RISC

D. HALs for Alpha AXP

E. All of the above

A, B, and D are the correct answers

Question ID: 85

You are a network administrator responsible for upgrading your company's Intel-based computers from an older version of Windows NT Workstation to version 4.0. Which installation method is preferable in this situation?

    A. WINNT32.EXE from the Network

    B. WINNT.EXE from the CD-ROM

    C. Boot Installation

    D. SETUPLDR

    E. Delete the old installation and re-install using Windows NT v4.0.

A is the correct answer

Question ID: 87

What happens when you run WINNT /OX ?

    A. It installs Windows NT on the workstation.

    B. It provides support for Proprietary HALs.

    C. It sets up the NTFS file system.

    D. It installs Windows NT on the server.

    E. It creates a new set of setup diskettes.

E is the correct answer

Question ID: 88

Installing Windows NT Workstation on a RISC-based system requires a _____ as the installation source.

    A. Network

    B. Floppy Drive

    C. Previous copy of NT

    D. Local CD-ROM

    E. Local Hard Drive

D is the correct answer

Question ID: 89

Which of the following statements regarding upgrading from another Windows product to Windows NT Workstation v4.0 are true?

   A.   You can upgrade from Windows 95 by installing Windows NT in the same directory.
   B.   Current Windows settings are automatically migrated.
   C.   Existing program groups and applications are migrated.
   D.   Install Windows NT in a separate directory from the current Windows application to support dual-boot.
   E.   Windows NT will not install if there is not a network present.

B, C, and D are the correct answers

Question ID: 90

Which of the following tasks are accomplished during the Windows NT setup process?

   A.   The system will search for mass storage devices.
   B.   You must agree with the client licensing agreement.
   C.   You have the opportunity to modify existing partitions.
   D.   You will give your system a unique NetBIOS name.
   E.   You will be prompted to create groups.

A, B, C, and D are the correct answers

Question ID: 91

You have just finished installing Windows NT on a co-worker's computer. You now need to create an Emergency Repair Diskette. Which utility would you use?

   A.   COMMAND.COM
   B.   REGEDIT.EXE
   C.   RDISK.EXE
   D.   REPAIR.EXE
   E.   WINNT /OX

C is the correct answer

Question ID: 92

When is the Windows NT System Administrator account created?

- A. During the Windows NT setup process.
- B. The first time the administrator logs onto the system.
- C. Before you begin the Windows NT setup process.
- D. When the Windows NT installation process is completed.
- E. When you manually create the account using the User Manager utility.

A is the correct answer

Question ID: 93

Select the valid NetBIOS names from the list below.

- A. John's Computer
- B. OFFICE213
- C. 14THFLOORCOMPUTER
- D. PHONE5551212
- E. These are all valid NETBIOS names.

B and D are the correct answers

Question ID: 94

Which of the following protocols are provided in the default Network Selections dialog box for Windows NT?

- A. TCP/IP
- B. DLC Protocol
- C. IPX/SPX
- D. NetBEUI
- E. AppleTalk

A, C, and D are the correct answers

Question ID: 95

You are running the WINNT installation from an MS-DOS prompt under Windows. What startup switch is required?

A.   /B
B.   /W
C.   /F
D.   /DW
E.   /X

B is the correct answer

Question ID: 96

What is the first step of the Windows NT startup sequence?

A.   NTLDR
B.   Hardware Detection
C.   Boot Record Load
D.   Kernel Load
E.   None of the above

C is the correct answer

Question ID: 97

What happens when the kernel initialization is successful under Windows NT?

A.   CHKDSK is run on all hard disk partitions.
B.   The Registry System hive is loaded.
C.   The processor is placed in 32-bit flat memory mode.
D.   The Windows NT logo screen appears.
E.   All of the above

A and D are the correct answers

Question ID: 98

Select the true statements from below.

    A. Logging on to a Windows NT workstation requires a valid user account name and password.

    B. Windows NT passwords are case-insensitive.

    C. Logging on to a Windows NT workstation activates the security sub-system.

    D. If you are part of a Windows NT Server domain, you must log on to your local station and the domain separately.

A and C are the correct answers

Question ID: 99

You are in charge of computer security for your organization and you are developing a new policy for all computer users. Your company uses Windows NT Workstation v4.0 on all computer workstations. When the employees take their lunch break, which action below will assure that their systems remain secure?

    A. Shut down the system.

    B. Lock the workstation.

    C. Log off the computer.

    D. Change the password.

    E. Disconnect the keyboard.

B is the correct answer

Question ID: 100

What happens when you log off a Windows NT workstation?

    A. All application sessions are ended.

    B. Background services and shared resources remain running.

    C. The operating system remains active.

    D. Any buffered data in memory is written to disk.

    E. The computer is automatically powered down.

A, B, and C are the correct answers

Question ID: 191

Windows NT Workstation supports all of the following processors EXCEPT:

    A.   PowerPC processors.

    B.   Alpha AXP processors.

    C.   MIPS R4x00 processors.

    D.   Intel 80486 processors.

    E.   Intel 80386 processors.

E is the correct answer

Question ID: 193

Which statements about Windows NT installation are true?

    A.   Use WINNT, WINNT32, or SETUPLDR to install Windows NT on a RISC platform.

    B.   WINNT /OX can create the installation boot floppies if they are misplaced.

    C.   On the installation CD-ROM, run WINNT or WINNT32 from the /ALPHA directory to install on an Alpha AXP-based system.

    D.   On the installation CD-ROM, run WINNT or WINNT32 from the /INTEL directory to install on an Intel-based system.

    E.   To upgrade a Windows NT v3.51 system to Windows NT v4.0, use WINNT32 to perform the upgrade installation.

B, C, and E are the correct answers

Question ID: 194

The HAL:

A. Is the Hidden Application Layer that prevents unauthorized applications to be installed on a Windows NT system.

B. Is the Hardware Access Level that defines the capabilities of the currently logged on user to access attached hardware devices on a Windows NT Workstation.

C. Is the Host Activation Liaison that is used on Windows NT-based Web servers to validate authorized users.

D. Is the Host Authorization Link that provides security database replication between servers in a Windows NT domain.

E. Is the Hardware Abstraction Layer that interfaces the Windows NT operating system to the computer hardware.

E is the correct answer

Question ID: 195

A customer calls with a question regarding the installation of Windows NT Workstation. They wish to upgrade their current Windows 95 installation to the NT platform. What should you caution them to do prior to beginning the upgrade?

A. Assure that all current shortcuts on the Start Menu are valid. Delete all invalid shortcuts prior to beginning the upgrade.

B. Remove any MS-DOS based programs from the system prior to beginning the upgrade.

C. Run the Windows NT Upgrade Wizard from Windows 95 to identify any hardware that is not supported by Windows NT.

D. Back up their current installation in case they need to "back out" of Windows NT installation.

E. Run the FDISK program to convert all FAT partitions to NTFS prior to beginning the upgrade.

D is the correct answer

Question ID: 196

A customer calls with a question regarding the installation of Windows NT Workstation. They wish to install Windows NT to dual-boot with their current Windows 95 installation. What do they need to do to accomplish this?

    A.   Install Windows NT into the same directory as Windows 95.

    B.   Install Windows NT into a new directory and edit the BOOT.INI file by placing the statement BOOTMULTI=1 at the end of the file.

    C.   Install Windows NT into a new directory. The system will automatically configure itself for dual-booting.

    D.   Install Windows NT into the same directory as Windows 95 and edit the MSDOS.SYS file to include the line BOOTMULTI=1.

    E.   Tell the customer that you cannot configure this system to dual boot. You must install Windows NT before Windows 95 to enable this feature.

C is the correct answer

Question ID: 197

You need to perform an emergency repair of a Windows NT installation. You have booted from the Windows NT setup floppy disks to begin the process. Which key combination will initiate the emergency repair sequence from the Welcome to Setup screen?

    A.   <F1>

    B.   <ENTER>

    C.   <R>

    D.   <F3>

    E.   You cannot initiate the emergency repair sequence when you boot from the Windows NT setup floppy disks.

C is the correct answer

Question ID: 198

Which of the following statements about the Windows NT installation are true?

A. The setup program will attempt to detect all mass storage devices, such as CD-ROM drives and SCSI devices.

B. If you do not agree with the license agreement, installation will continue but you must add client access licenses as soon as setup completes.

C. Windows NT must be installed in the \WINNT directory.

D. Windows NT setup will convert the boot partition to NTFS by default, you must intervene by pressing N when prompted to avoid this.

E. You must have a formatted partition on your hard drive prior to installing Windows NT.

A is the correct answer

Question ID: 199

A customer calls with a problem logging onto their Windows NT Workstation v4.0 computer. Which of the following questions would be pertinent to ask the customer in order to troubleshoot the problem?

A. Are you typing in your password in the appropriate case? Windows NT passwords are case-sensitive.

B. Are you typing in your username in the appropriate case? Windows NT usernames are case-sensitive.

C. Are there time restrictions on the user's account? If so, what times are allowed for logon?

D. Is the workstation participating in a Windows NT domain? If so, do you have the correct domain name entered?

E. What is the error message? Windows NT provides very specific messages if a logon fails.

A, C, and D are the correct answers

Question ID: 200

A customer calls asking you how to uninstall Windows NT Workstation v4.0 from a computer. You should direct the customer to do each of the following steps EXCEPT:

A. Boot the system from an MS-DOS system diskette.
B. Use the ATTRIB command to remove the system, hidden, and read-only attributes from BOOT.INI, NTDETECT.COM, and NTLDR and then delete these files.
C. Use the ATTRIB command to remove the system, hidden, and read-only attributes from BOOT.INI, MSDOS.SYS, IO.SYS, NTDETECT.COM, and NTLDR and then delete these files.
D. Run the SYS command to transfer MS-DOS system files to the hard disk.
E. Format the hard drive.

C and E are the correct answers

Question ID: 288

What is the minimum suggested memory when installing Windows NT Workstation v4.0 on an Intel x86 platform?

A. 8 MB
B. 12 MB
C. 16 MB
D. 20 MB
E. 24 MB

B is the correct answer

Question ID: 289

What is the minimum suggested hard disk space for installing Windows NT Workstation v4.0 on an Intel x86 platform?

A. 30 MB
B. 40 MB
C. 75 MB
D. 92 MB
E. 117 MB

E is the correct answer

Question ID: 290

What is the minimum suggested free hard disk space when installing Windows NT Workstation v4.0 on a RISC-based platform?

    A. 30 MB

    B. 40 MB

    C. 75 MB

    D. 92 MB

    E. 124 MB

E is the correct answer

Question ID: 291

What installation method is used when installing Windows NT Workstation v4.0 on a RISC-based system?

    A. Floppy diskette

    B. Local CD-ROM

    C. SCSI tape

    D. Network file server

    E. Any of the above will work

B is the correct answer

Question ID: 292

When installing Windows NT Workstation v4.0 from a Windows v3.1 system with an unsupported CD-ROM, what command do you run to start the installation?

    A. SETUP

    B. NTSETUP

    C. WINNT

    D. WIN40

    E. CDINST

C is the correct answer

Question ID: 293

You are installing Windows NT Workstation on an existing MS-DOS machine and want to be able to boot DOS. After selecting the system's only disk partition as the destination, you should:

A. Convert to NTFS.
B. Reformat to NTFS.
C. Reformat to FAT.
D. Keep the existing file system intact.
E. None of the above

D is the correct answer

Question ID: 294

A user on a Pentium-processor machine with 32 MB of RAM needs to run resource-intensive statistical programs in the background while generating complicated graphics in the foreground. The user will not be connected to a network. You should install:

A. MS-DOS v6.22
B. Windows v3.1
C. Windows for Workgroups v3.11
D. Windows NT Workstation v4.0
E. Windows NT Server v4.0

D is the correct answer

Question ID: 295

What is the minimum suggested memory when installing Windows NT Workstation on a RISC system?

A. 8 MB
B. 12 MB
C. 24 MB
D. 32 MB
E. 64 MB

D is the correct answer

Question ID: 296

Which of the following are required for RISC installation of Windows NT Workstation v4.0?

    A. High-density 3.5-in. floppy disk drive
    B. Supported CD-ROM drive and adapter
    C. Math coprocessor
    D. VGA adapter and driver
    E. Sound Card

B and D are the correct answers

Question ID: 298

Your disk is currently set up as FAT. You want to save all of the files and to be able to use MS-DOS file utilities. You are not concerned about local security, but need long filename support. What file system should you use?

    A. FAT
    B. HPFS
    C. NTFS
    D. Any of the above
    E. None of the above

A is the correct answer

Question ID: 299

You are installing Windows NT Workstation on a new system with no operating system currently installed. Your primary concern is local security. Which file system should you use?

    A. FAT
    B. HPFS
    C. NTFS
    D. AFP
    E. Any of the above

C is the correct answer

Question ID: 300

Which of the following are valid Windows NT Workstation v4.0 installation sources for an Intel x86-based system?

    A. Supported CD-ROM

    B. Unsupported CD-ROM

    C. Network Server

    D. SCSI tape

    E. All of the above

A, B, and C are the correct answers

Question ID: 301

Which of the following are valid Windows NT Workstation v4.0 installation sources for a RISC-based system?

    A. Supported CD-ROM

    B. Unsupported CD-ROM

    C. Network Server

    D. SCSI tape

    E. All of the above

A is the correct answer

Question ID: 302

What is the command name used to initiate a new installation of Windows NT Workstation on a RISC-based platform?

    A. INSTALL

    B. SETUP

    C. SETUPLDR

    D. WINNT

    E. WINNT32

C is the correct answer

Question ID: 303

You are installing Windows NT Workstation from an unsupported CD-ROM. You do NOT plan to generate an emergency repair diskette. How many formatted diskettes will you need to run the installation?

    A. 1
    B. 2
    C. 3
    D. 4
    E. 5

C is the correct answer

Question ID: 304

To uninstall Windows NT Workstation, you must:

    A. Run MS-DOS setup to reinstall all MS-DOS files.
    B. Reformat the Windows NT Workstation Partition.
    C. Delete BOOT.INI, NTDETECT.COM, and NTLDR from the root directory.
    D. Run SYS C: from an MS-DOS system diskette.
    E. Delete all data files created after Windows NT Workstation installation.

C and D are the correct answers

Question ID: 306

What happens when you press <CTRL><ALT><DEL> when working under Windows NT Workstation v4.0?

    A. The logon (Welcome) dialog is displayed.
    B. You get a message asking if you want to terminate your Windows NT session.
    C. The system resets.
    D. The security dialog is displayed.
    E. The system prompts to verify before resetting.

D is the correct answer

Question ID: 307

What happens when you select Lock Workstation from the Security dialog?

    A.   No files are closed.

    B.   Background applications are suspended.

    C.   All active services are closed.

    D.   The keyboard is completely disabled.

    E.   All outstanding print jobs are deleted.

A is the correct answer

Question ID: 308

How can you modify the amount of time the boot loader menu is displayed in Windows NT Workstation v4.0?

    A.   Control Panel System Utility

    B.   Control Panel Server Utility

    C.   Directly edit BOOT.INI.

    D.   Directly edit NTLDR.

    E.   The value cannot be changed.

A and C are the correct answers

Question ID: 309

Which of the following are Windows NT system startup files?

    A.   NTLDR

    B.   BOOT.EXE

    C.   NTDETECT.COM

    D.   COMMAND.COM

    E.   LOAD.COM

A and C are the correct answers

Question ID: 310

Which of the following statements about BOOT.INI are true in Windows NT Workstation v4.0?

    A. It is stored in the Windows NT Workstation directory, normally WINNT.

    B. It is an ASCII text file and can be modified with any text editor.

    C. It sets the length of time the boot loader menu displays.

    D. It only exists if the system already had MS-DOS loaded before installing Windows NT.

    E. It can be deleted without affecting startup.

B and C are the correct answers

Question ID: 311

What is the purpose of pressing <CTRL><ALT><DEL> at the Welcome screen after startup in Windows NT Workstation v4.0?

    A. It clears the previous username.

    B. It automatically scans the disk and reorganizes files.

    C. It causes a system interrupt and thus deters virus infections.

    D. It resets all Windows NT applications to defaults.

    E. It activates the security subsystem.

C and E are the correct answers

Question ID: 312

Which of the following are valid security dialog selections?

    A. Change password

    B. Lock workstation

    C. End task

    D. Restart system

    E. Shut down

A, B, and E are the correct answers

Question ID: 313

NTLDR is able to start up a Windows NT Workstation v4.0 system from:

A. A FAT partition.

B. A SCSI tape.

C. An NTFS partition.

D. A CD-ROM.

E. All of the above

A and C are the correct answers

Question ID: 316

You want to create a Windows NT Workstation v4.0 boot diskette for an Intel x86 system with an IDE drive. Which of the following files will you need?

A. NTLDR

B. BOOT.INI

C. NTDETECT.COM

D. NTBOOT.SYS

E. WINNT.EXE

A, B, and C are the correct answers

Question ID: 318

In Windows NT Workstation v4.0, all open files and applications are closed when:

A. You lock a workstation.

B. You log off from a workstation.

C. You shut down a workstation.

D. An application error occurs in an MS-DOS application session.

E. The virtual memory paging file is dynamically increased.

B and C are the correct answers

Question ID: 332

You have chosen to install Windows NT Workstation because of the security it provides. Prior to installation, you have to make sure that all systems meet at least the minimum requirements for installation. Which of the following is not part of your minimum hardware requirements list?

    A. Hard disk drives

    B. Pointing devices

    C. Network adapters

    D. Processors

    E. Memory

B is the correct answer

Question ID: 333

A small local company uses RISC-based systems for most of its applications. Some systems are currently running Windows NT. The company has now decided to install Windows NT Workstation on all of its RISC systems. What method should they use for installation?

    A. Boot from installation diskettes.

    B. Run SETUPLDR.

    C. Run WINNT or WINNT32 from the network server.

    D. Install directly from CD-ROM.

B and D are the correct answers

Question ID: 334

You are currently running Windows 95 on you system. You decide to install Windows NT Workstation from the network server and run WINNT32. You do not want to create boot floppies, as they were created for you earlier. What WINNT32 option switch will let you bypass creation of boot floppies?

    A. /ox

    B. /x

    C. /t:drive

    D. /u:drive

    E. /u

B is the correct answer

Question ID: 335

You booted from the installation diskette and started a Windows NT Workstation installation. After completing mass storage detection and agreeing to client licensing, you are prompted to select the Workstation destination. You want to create a new partition in unpartitioned space on your hard drive. What would you do?

    A. Press <N>

    B. Press <ENTER>

    C. Press <D>

    D. Press <C>

D is the correct answer

Question ID: 336

After completing the text-based portion of the Windows NT Workstation installation, you have entered the graphic mode. You need to install only those files which are needed to set up and run Windows NT Workstation while minimizing disk space requirements. Which of the following options should you choose?

    A. Portable

    B. Compact

    C. Typical

    D. Custom

B is the correct answer

Question ID: 337

After completing the text-based portion of installation, you entered the graphic mode. You have a system with no special needs or hardware concerns and want to keep user interaction to a minimum during installation. You want the most common Windows NT Workstation features installed. Which Setup Option should you select?

    A. Compact
    B. Custom
    C. Typical
    D. Portable

C is the correct answer

Question ID: 338

You want to install certain selected components and services, such as Chat, Hyperterminal, and Internet Mail. You want as much direct control over the installation process as possible. Which option should you select?

    A. Custom
    B. Compact
    C. Typical
    D. Portable

A is the correct answer

Question ID: 339

After completing the installation on your Intel x86, you are now ready to run and use Windows NT Workstation. When you boot the system, you are given the choice between running Windows NT Workstation or MS-DOS. In what file is the information used to build this menu stored?

    A. BOOT.INI
    B. BOOTSECT.DOS
    C. NTDETECT.COM
    D. NTOSKRNL.EXE

A is the correct answer

Question ID: 340

From time to time Tom has to leave his desk for a short period. Other times he has to go to a client office, which is just a couple of blocks away. Tom works with confidential information related to the company and his clients. What should he do to protect his Windows NT Workstation system from unauthorized access, but still keep background applications running while he is gone?

    A.   Change his password every time he leaves his desk.

    B.   Log off his system every time he leaves his desk.

    C.   Lock his Workstation when he leaves his desk.

    D.   Shut down the system when he leaves his desk.

    E.   None of the above

C is the correct answer

Question ID: 344

You are installing Windows NT Workstation on a Windows for Workgroups system. You want to be able to run a dual boot with MS-DOS after installation. What file system should you use on the destination partition to install Windows NT to the boot partition?

    A.   NTFS

    B.   FAT

    C.   HPFS

    D.   CDFS

B is the correct answer

Question ID: 345

You are responsible for purchasing a new system for your company which will run Windows NT Workstation. What are the minimum requriements of the system you purchase?

    A.   Pentium Processor, 250 MB disk space, 16 MB RAM

    B.   486 Processor, 150 MB disk space, 12 MB RAM

    C.   486 Processor, 120 MB disk space, 12 MB RAM

    D.   486 Processor, 130 MB disk space, 16 MB RAM

C is the correct answer

Question ID: 346

Your company has been running Windows 95 exclusively, but now wishes to install Windows NT Workstation on half of its systems. Windows 95 will no longer be needed on the systems that have NT, which will be used for critical projects involving highly sensitive data. Each system has a single disk partition. What file system should you select during installation?

- A. NTFS
- B. FAT
- C. HPFS
- D. CDFS

A is the correct answer

Question ID: 347

You have an Intel x86 system with two 1-GB hard disks and an internal CD-ROM. You cannot read the Windows NT boot diskettes and suspect a problem with the floppy disk drive. You do not have time to replace the drive. How can you install Windows NT?

- A. Run WINNT /B from the CD-ROM.
- B. Run WINNT /OX to create new diskettes.
- C. Run WINNT over the network.
- D. First install Windows 95 on the hard drive and then install Windows NT Workstation.

A is the correct answer

Question ID: 355

Which of the following statements are FALSE about Windows NT domains?

- A. Each domain requires the presence of a Primary Domain Controller.
- B. Windows NT Workstations can serve as a Primary Domain Controller.
- C. Windows NT Workstations must participate in a domain.
- D. All Windows NT Servers in a domain share the same user account database.
- E. Users in a domain are assigned rights to network resources based on their user account.

B and C are the correct answers

NAVIGATING THE USER INTERFACE

For review of this topic refer to Chapter 8.

Question ID: 101

Which of the following Windows NT v3.5 components does the Windows NT v4.0 Explorer replace?

    A. Program Manager
    B. Print Manager
    C. Task Manager
    D. File Manager
    E. Network Neighborhood

A, B, and D are the correct answers

Question ID: 102

You have several employees sharing one computer running Windows NT Workstation v4.0. Each employee has their own screen savers, sounds, and other environmental settings. Which Windows NT directory stores individual user desktop configurations associated with their login name?

    A. WINNT\PROFILES
    B. WINNT\PROFILES\username\DESKTOP
    C. WINNT\PROFILES\DESKTOP
    D. WINNT\
    E. WINDOWS\DESKTOP\PROFILES

B is the correct answer

Question ID: 103

Which of the following Windows NT Workstation v4.0 desktop objects allows you to view all members of your workgroup and domain?

   A. My Computer
   B. My Briefcase
   C. Network Neighborhood
   D. Microsoft Exchange
   E. Microsoft Network (MSN)

C is the correct answer

Question ID: 104

By clicking the secondary mouse button on the Windows NT desktop and selecting Properties, which of the following elements can you modify?

   A. Screen Saver
   B. Color Schemes
   C. Network Passwords
   D. Start Menu Applications
   E. Desktop Icon Appearance

A, B, and E are the correct answers

Question ID: 105

Brad has called you seeking assistance in configuring his task bar on his Windows NT workstation. Using the Start menu, which menu option would you have Brad select?

   A. Open
   B. Programs
   C. Documents
   D. Settings
   E. Customize

D is the correct answer

Question ID: 107

Which of the following methods for accessing the Windows NT Workstation v4.0 Control Panel will display the Control Panel utilities in the Explorer Contents window?

    A. Launch Control Panel from the "My Computer" window.

    B. Run Settings from the Start menu and select Control Panel.

    C. Select Run from the Start menu and type CONTROL.

    D. None of the above

C is the correct answer

Question ID: 108

When noting the differences between Windows v3.1 initialization files and the Registry, which of the following are correct?

    A. The .INI files holds more information than the registry files.

    B. The registry holds more information than .INI files.

    C. The registry is formatted differently.

    D. Registry entries must follow a precise format.

    E. The Registry is only one file, but there are several .INI files.

B, C, and D are the correct answers

Question ID: 110

Select the information passed on to the Registry from other Windows NT system components.

    A. Configuration information from Setup and application installations.

    B. Kernel information during startup.

    C. Hardware detected during startup.

    D. Device driver system resources.

    E. All of the above

E is the correct answer

Question ID: 112

The Registry is physically organized into _____, which contain the keys, subkeys, and values for the registry.

    A. Sub-trees
    B. Registry Parameters
    C. Rows and Columns
    D. Directories
    E. Hives

E is the correct answer

Question ID: 114

What are the components of each Windows NT Registry value entry?

    A. Name
    B. Data Type
    C. Key
    D. Hive
    E. Value

A, B, and E are the correct answers

Question ID: 115

All of the following statements regarding Windows NT value entries are correct except:

    A. The value size can be up to 1 MB, except for REG_DWORD.
    B. Value entries are never case-sensitive.
    C. Name values are Unicode character strings.
    D. The value can contain arbitrary data strings and raw binary data.

B is the correct answer

Question ID: 116

You need to modify the Registry entries on your Windows NT workstation. Select the recommended method of accomplishing this.

A. Create a shortcut for REGEDIT on your desktop.
B. Edit the Registry indirectly through standard system utilities.
C. Run REGEDIT.EXE from the Start menu.
D. Open REGEDIT in Notepad.
E. Open REGEDIT in the DOS EDIT utility.

B is the correct answer

Question ID: 134

What key combination executes the Cool Switch in Windows NT?

A. <ALT><TAB>
B. <CTRL><ALT>
C. <ESC>
D. <CTRL><ALT><DELETE>
E. <ALT><F1>

A is the correct answer

Question ID: 176

Which of the following statements about shortcuts are TRUE in Windows NT Workstation v4.0?

A. If the target to a shortcut has moved since the creation of the shortcut, Windows 95 will attempt to locate the missing target the next time the shortcut is used.
B. Shortcuts have the MS-DOS filename extension of SHC.
C. A shortcut does not have properties.
D. Global information about each shortcut on a system is stored in the \WINDOWS\SHORTCUT directory.
E. Shortcuts to network resources cannot be created.

A and B are the correct answers

Question ID: 201

By default on a computer running Windows NT Workstation v4.0, the
_____ directory stores individual user desktop configurations
associated with their login name.

    A. \WINDOWS\DESKTOP

    B. \WINNT\DESKTOP

    C. \WINDOWS\PROFILES\username\DESKTOP

    D. \WINNT\PROFILES\username\DESKTOP

D is the correct answer

Question ID: 202

By default, where are the Windows NT Registry files stored?

    A. \WINNT\HIVES

    B. \WINNT\SYSTEM\CONFIG

    C. \WINNT\CONFIG

    D. \WINNT\SYSTEM32\CONFIG

    E. \WINNT\REGISTRY

D is the correct answer

Question ID: 203

By default, the Windows NT Registry supports all of the following data types EXCEPT:

    A. REG_BINARY

    B. REG_TEXT

    C. REG_DWORD

    D. REG_SZ

    E. REG_MULTI_SZ

B is the correct answer

Question ID: 204

Windows NT provides two programs for viewing and directly modifying the contents of the Registry. These are:

  A. POLEDIT.EXE
  B. REGEDT32.EXE
  C. REGEDIT.EXE
  D. SYSEDIT.EXE
  E. EDIT.COM

B and C are the correct answers

Question ID: 205

A customer calls with a question. They wish to make a copy of their registry files on their Windows NT Workstation v4.0 computer. Which of the following procedures will allow them to accomplish this?

  A. Use the Registry Editor to export the registry to a text file.
  B. Use the Windows NT Backup program to copy the registry files to a diskette.
  C. Using the Explorer, locate the \WINNT\SYSTEM32\CONFIG directory. Copy these files to a diskette or alternate location.
  D. Boot the system from an MS-DOS system diskette. Copy the files located in the \WINNT\SYSTEM32\CONFIG directory to a diskette or alternate location.
  E. Use the Windows NT Backup program to copy the registry files to a supported tape drive.

A, D, and E are the correct answers

Question ID: 269

Select the true statements regarding the Windows NT Workstation v4.0 Registry.

  A. Any user can edit the registry.
  B. System changes should be made through the system utilities that modify registry values.
  C. Use the Registry Editor to directly edit registry key values when necessary.
  D. The registry cannot be directly edited.
  E. Keys can only be deleted indirectly, through the Control Panel.

B and C are the correct answers

Question ID: 275

To manage local file access permissions under Windows NT Workstation v4.0, the
_____ utility is used.

    A. User Manager

    B. Explorer

    C. Control Panel Security

    D. Disk Administrator

    E. None of the above will work.

B is the correct answer

Question ID: 314

Which of the following Windows NT Workstation v4.0 utilities lets you update the
Emergency Repair Diskette?

    A. DISKFIX

    B. Explorer

    C. RDISK

    D. ERDISKFX

C is the correct answer

Question ID: 315

In Windows NT Workstation v4.0, you can run _____ to create an Emergency
Repair Diskette.

    A. MAKEERD

    B. RDISK

    C. EDISK

    D. FIXDISK

    E. ERD

B is the correct answer

WINDOWS NT HARDWARE MANAGEMENT

For review of this topic refer to Chapter 9.

Question ID: 118

Which of the following actions will optimize swap file performance under Windows NT?

    A.   Put the swap file on the same physical hard disk as the system files.

    B.   Spread the swap file across multiple physical drives.

    C.   Monitor swap file size over a period of time. If you can determine a typical swap file size, use this as your guideline for modifying the file size.

    D.   Set up both permanent and temporary swap files.

    E.   All of the above

B and C are the correct answers

Question ID: 122

There are several ways to access the Printers properties in a Windows NT workstation. Select the correct methods from those listed below.

    A.   Select Printers from the Settings option in the Start menu.

    B.   Open the Printers folder from the My Computer icon.

    C.   Select Run from the Start menu and type PRINTERS.

    D.   Double-click on the Printers object located in Control Panel.

    E.   Right-click on the desktop and select Printers from the drop down menu that appears.

A, B, and D are the correct answers

Question ID: 123

You have two identical printers that you have attached to a Windows NT Workstation. You wish to have them appear as one printer to users browsing the network with the Network Neighborhood. Windows NT will then service a print queue using these two printers. What do you have to do when setting up these printers to allow this?

    A. Connect the printers to the same LPT port.

    B. Use the same print driver for both printers.

    C. Enable printer pooling.

    D. Use the same descriptive name for both printers.

    E. You cannot do this with Windows NT Workstation. You must install Windows NT Server to accomplish this.

C is the correct answer

Question ID: 125

You can use Windows NT Disk Administrator to:

    A. Create disk partitions and logical drives.

    B. Delete logical drives.

    C. Assign drive IDs.

    D. Format a partition using either FAT or NTFS.

    E. Disable hard drives.

A, B, C, and D are the correct answers

Question ID: 128

You are attempting to gather information from a Windows NT Workstation user over the phone. You need to walk her through launching the Windows NT Diagnostics utility. Select the instructions you would give her from those listed below.

    A. Select Run from the Start Menu and type WINNTDIAG.

    B. Select Run from the Start Menu and type MSD.

    C. Click on the NT Diagnostics objecct in the Control Panel.

    D. Select Run from the Start Menu and type WINMSD.

    E. Right-click on the System object in the Control Panel and select NT Diagnostics from the drop-down menu that appears.

D is the correct answer

Question ID: 207

Which of the following statements about Windows NT virtual memory and swap files are true?

A. You can set the initial size, maximum size, and location of the swap file.
B. You can improve performance of a Windows NT computer by spreading the swap file across multiple logical drives on a single physical drive.
C. Current Windows NT virtual memory usage can be viewed by using WINMSD.
D. The swap file is named PAGEFILE.SYS.
E. You can only place the swap file on the primary, or C: drive.

A, C, and D are the correct answers

Question ID: 208

Under Windows NT Workstation v4.0, device drivers have all of the following configuration options EXCEPT:

A. Boot
B. System
C. User
D. Automatic
E. Disabled

C is the correct answer

Question ID: 209

A customer calls with a problem. They inadvertently changed the display settings to a higher resolution than their monitor can support. Now, they see various wavering lines of color when they start Windows NT. Due to this, they cannot change their settings back to the original configuration. What would be the most appropriate course of action to fix this problem?

A. Restore the system from the most recent backup.

B. Reinstall Windows NT.

C. Restart the system and select "Windows NT Workstation Version 4.00 [VGA Mode]" at startup and change the display settings.

D. Boot from an MS-DOS system diskette and run the command line REGEDIT. Change the display settings in the HKEY_LOCAL_MACHINE\DISPLAY hive.

E. Check all monitor cables to assure that they are connected correctly.

C is the correct answer

Question ID: 210

Which of the following statements about Windows NT printing support are false?

A. Windows NT does not support printers attached to the serial port.

B. If you share a printer attached to a Windows NT computer to the network, you will be prompted to select the operating systems that will be printing to this printer.

C. A Windows NT Workstation can be configured to print to a NetWare print queue.

D. Windows NT allows printer pooling where two or more printers attached to the computer are viewed as a single printer by network users.

E. All printer drivers that work under Windows 95 will work under Windows NT Workstation v4.0.

A and E are the correct answers

Question ID: 211

Which of the following statements about the Windows NT Disk Administrator are true?

A. The Disk Administrator allows you to format a partition using FAT, NTFS, or HPFS.
B. The Disk Administrator allows you to create or delete disk partitions and logical drives.
C. The Disk Administrator displays information about floppy disks.
D. The Disk Administrator allows you to change the drive letter used for a partition, logical drive, or CD-ROM.
E. The Disk Administrator displays information about redirected network drives.

B and D are the correct answers

Question ID: 268

What utility is used to install and remove an uninterruptable power supply support?

A. DRVINST.EXE
B. Disk Manager
C. Control Panel
D. Windows NT Setup
E. Fault Manager

C is the correct answer

Question ID: 271

What utility lets you change display driver configuration values?

A. Control Panel System
B. Control Panel Display
C. Windows NT Setup
D. System Manager
E. Control Panel Services

B is the correct answer

Question ID: 273

Windows NT Workstation is installed on an NTFS partition. How can you back up registry information?

    A. Boot from MS-DOS and copy the files.

    B. Boot from OS/2 and copy the files.

    C. Run RDISK to update the Emergency Repair Diskette.

    D. Run Backup and back up to tape.

    E. You cannot back up the Registry.

C and D are the correct answers

Question ID: 274

You have Windows NT Workstation installed on an NTFS partition. The Registry is corrupted and the system will not boot. Assuming it was backed up, how can you recover the Registry?

    A. Boot from a boot diskette and recover from tape.

    B. Boot from MS-DOS and recover from diskette.

    C. Boot from tape and recover.

    D. Boot from the Windows NT Workstation Setup diskettes and recover from the Emergency Repair Diskette.

    E. The Registry cannot be recovered by these methods.

D is the correct answer

Question ID: 281

What is a printer pool?

    A. One printer name sending output to multiple printers.

    B. Multiple printer names sending output to the same printer.

    C. Printers that can be used as network shares only.

    D. Virtual printers that print to a file.

    E. None of the above

A is the correct answer

Question ID: 282

Which of the following are valid Performance Monitor views?

    A. Chart
    B. Log
    C. Report
    D. Exception
    E. Comparison

A, B, and C are the correct answers

Question ID: 283

Which Performance Monitor view provides current numeric values for selected counters?

    A. Chart
    B. Log
    C. Alert
    D. Report
    E. None of the above

D is the correct answer

Question ID: 284

Which Performance Monitor view is used for storing information for later analysis?

    A. Chart
    B. Log
    C. Report
    D. Alert
    E. None of the above

B is the correct answer

Question ID: 285

In Windows NT Workstation, what should you monitor to determine which applications are placing the greatest load on the processor?

A. Disk activity
B. Active processes
C. Memory cache size
D. Active threads
E. RAM usage percentage

B and D are the correct answers

Question ID: 286

How can you improve the performance of the virtual memory paging file under Windows NT Workstation v4.0?

A. Decrease the minimum size of the file.
B. Place the paging file on the same partition as the Windows NT boot files.
C. Spread the paging file across multiple physical drives.
D. Spread the paging file across multiple logical drives.
E. Boot to MS-DOS and delete the paging file there.

C is the correct answer

Question ID: 305

What is the purpose of setting up a printer pool?

A. The user can select another printer if the primary printer is not on line.
B. If one printer is busy, the job will automatically be routed to the next available printer.
C. The user can select another printer if the printout is to be retreived from a remote location.
D. The user is prompted to choose a different printer is the selected printer is busy.
E. The printer pool is a list of all printers available to a workstation.

B is the correct answer

Question ID: 350

After adding a drive, you have started Disk Administrator for the first time. Next, you want to define a primary disk partition and then format the partition without having to shut down and restart the system. Which of the following methods should you choose for your requirements?

A. Run Create, then run Commit Change Now from the Partition menu before running Format from the Tools menu.

B. Run Create Extended from the Partition menu and then Format from the Disk menu.

C. Run Create Extended and then Commit Change Now from the Partition menu.

D. Run Create from the Partition menu and then Format from the Disk menu. The "Quick Format" box should be checked at this time.

A is the correct answer

WINDOWS NT SOFTWARE MANAGEMENT

For review of this topic refer to Chapter 10.

Question ID: 130

In _____, processor time is divided into time slices. The operating system is in control and time slices are assigned to applications according to their relative priority. This method gives the best performance and provides the most stable application environment.

A. Cooperative Multitasking
B. Multithreading
C. Symmetric Multiprocessing
D. Preemptive Multitasking
E. Thunking

D is the correct answer

Question ID: 131

Under Windows NT, 16-bit Windows applications use _____ to share the time allotted to a single WOW (Windows on Windows) session, unless you specify that the application should run in a separate address space.

A. Cooperative Multitasking
B. Multithreading
C. Symmetric Multiprocessing
D. Preemptive Multitasking
E. Virtual Memory

A is the correct answer

Question ID: 132

On a multiprocessor system, Windows NT uses _____ to schedule threads, thus allowing maximum performance from the processors.

A. Cooperative Multitasking
B. Multithreading
C. Symmetric Multiprocessing
D. Preemptive Multitasking
E. Processor Pooling

C is the correct answer

Question ID: 133

Select the command that gives you control over application priority and environment when launching an application from a command prompt or batch file.

A. Load
B. Run
C. Install
D. Control
E. Start

E is the correct answer

Question ID: 137

What command processor is used for the command prompt in Windows NT?

A. CMD.COM
B. COMMAND.EXE
C. CMD.EXE
D. NTCMD.EXE
E. CMDNT.EXE

C is the correct answer

Question ID: 138

Select the command symbol used to send the output of a command to a destination other than the display screen, such as a text file or a printer.

    A. |

    B. $

    C. *

    D. @

    E. >

E is the correct answer

Question ID: 139

When you launch a DOS application under Windows NT, what files are run to configure your DOS environment?

    A. CONFIG.SYS

    B. AUTOEXEC.NT

    C. AUTOEXEC.BAT

    D. CONFIG.NT

    E. COMMAND.COM

B and D are the correct answers

Question ID: 140

Which of the following components does Windows NT support for Win16 applications?

    A. Access to NTFS Files

    B. Full Data Exchange (OLE and Network OLE)

    C. Direct Access to system Hardware

    D. Windows v3.x Virtual Device Drivers

    E. All of the above

A and B are the correct answers

Question ID: 141

Which of the following are benefits of running a Win16 application in a separate memory space?

  A. It provides a higher level of security protection.
  B. It reduces processor requirements for application support.
  C. If the application becomes unstable, it won't affect other applications.
  D. It reduces memory requirements for applications support.

A and C are the correct answers

Question ID: 142

Under Windows NT Workstation, DOS applications run inside a _____ , which emulates the first megabyte of system memory.

  A. Window
  B. Virtual DOS Machine
  C. Virtual Memory Module
  D. Separate Processor Thread
  E. DOS Emulated Machine

B is the correct answer

Question ID: 169

Windows NT Workstation v4.0 includes the following features EXCEPT:

  A. Support for all legacy DOS-based applications.
  B. Support for Intel-based, ALPHA-based, and MIPS-based systems.
  C. DoD C2 Security compliance.
  D. Preemptive multitasking.
  E. Support for POSIX applications.

A is the correct answer

Question ID: 213

Windows NT supports the all of the following types of applications EXCEPT:

    A.   16-bit Windows applications.

    B.   32-bit Windows applications.

    C.   Macintosh System 7 applications.

    D.   OS/2 applications.

    E.   POSIX applications.

C is the correct answer

Question ID: 265

Your system provides non-critical file resources to the network. Its primary support is for active graphics editing. How should tasking be set?

    A.   The performance boost for the foreground application should be set to Maximum.

    B.   Foreground Application More Responsive than Background.

    C.   Foreground and Background Applications Equally Responsive.

    D.   Best background application Response Time.

    E.   It doesn't matter how they are set.

A is the correct answer

Question ID: 266

Windows NT Workstation supports what application types?

    A.   POSIX

    B.   MS-DOS

    C.   Win16

    D.   Macintosh

    E.   OS/2 Presentation Manager v2.x

B and C are the correct answers

Question ID: 267

What must be done to launch an MS-DOS application in a separate memory address space?

    A.   Create a special PIF for the application.
    B.   Launch using the START command with the /SPECIAL option.
    C.   Specify to run in separate memory space when launching from Explorer.
    D.   It is not necessary to do anything.

D is the correct answer

Question ID: 351

You have been working in the OS/2 subsystem environment and now you want to move ot another window. You also want to pass CMD.EXE startup environment information to this window. What START command should you use?

    A.   START /dpath
    B.   START /i
    C.   START /separate
    D.   START /realtime

B is the correct answer

Question ID: 352

You want to redirect output to a file and want that output to be appended to the file contents. Which of the following commands would you use?

    A.   sort < list.txt
    B.   chkdsk d: >> 0122chk.txt
    C.   dir > list.txt
    D.   cd temp_dir II md temp_dir

B is the correct answer

Question ID: 353

You want to have a command which will only run if the preceding command completes without error. What command operator would you use to separate the commands?

A. >

B. >>

C. II

D. &&

E. ()

D is the correct answer

WINDOWS NT USER AND SECURITY MANAGEMENT

For review of this topic refer to Chapter 11.

Question ID: 143

Select the characteristics of a domain.

    A. It is a logical group of devices on a network.

    B. Each resource has its own password.

    C. All servers in the domain share the same user account database.

    D. Users are assigned rights to network resources based on their user account.

    E. A new domain is created each time Windows NT Workstation is installed.

A, C, and D are the correct answers

Question ID: 144

You are creating a security policy for your company. Which of the following guidelines should be followed when creating user accounts?

    A. Allow each user to be the administrator of his/her own workstation.

    B. Let users share accounts to save time and space.

    C. Strictly limit the number of administrators.

    D. Limit rights to those required for the user to perform his duties.

    E. All of the above

C and D are the correct answers

Question ID: 145

You are training users on how to maintain a secure workstation. When covering the topic of passwords, which of the following would NOT be included in your password security checklist?

    A. Change your password frequently.

    B. Select an easy to remember password, such as your name.

    C. Do not leave passwords displayed in a visible location.

    D. Use nonsense characters and symbols.

    E. Do not use a password so that important data is accessible when you are away from the office.

B and E are the correct answers

Question ID: 146

Which file system must be implemented to take the full advantage of C2 security?

    A. NTFS

    B. FAT

    C. HPFS

    D. FAT32

A is the correct answer

Question ID: 148

You need to create user definitions for a Windows NT workstation. Select the utility you would use to perform this function.

    A. User Manager for Domains

    B. File Access Security

    C. Windows Explorer

    D. User Manager

    E. Network Neighborhood

D is the correct answer

Question ID: 149

Where is the User Manager utility located?

- A. Control Panel
- B. Administrative Tools in Start/Programs
- C. System Object
- D. Network Neighborhood
- E. Windows Explorer

B is the correct answer

Question ID: 150

Select the user accounts created during the Windows NT installation.

- A. Administrator
- B. Power User
- C. Anonymous
- D. System
- E. Guest

A and E are the correct answers

Question ID: 151

Select the true statements from below as they apply to Windows NT.

- A. Passwords and usernames are both case-sensitive.
- B. Passwords are not case-sensitive, while usernames are case-sensitive.
- C. Neither passwords nor usernames are case-sensitive.
- D. Passwords are case-sensitive, while usernames are not.

D is the correct answer

Question ID: 152

Assuming that Windows NT is installed in the default C:\WINNT directory, what is the default directory path for the home directory of the user BBROWN?

   A. C:\WINNT\SYSTEM32\PROFILES\ BBROWN \PERSONAL

   B. C:\PROFILES\ BBROWN \PERSONAL

   C. C:\WINNT\PROFILES\BBROWN\HOMEDIR

   D. C:\WINNT\PROFILES\ BBROWN \PERSONAL

   E. C:\WINNT\BBROWN

B is the correct answer

Question ID: 153

Which of the following values are set in the User Environmental Profile dialog box?

   A. User Profile Path

   B. User Password

   C. Login Script

   D. Home Directory

   E. Group Memberships

A, C, and D are the correct answers

Question ID: 155

Once a user profile has been created, which of the following fields cannot be modified on the User Properties screen?

   A. Description

   B. Password

   C. Username

   D. Full Name

C is the correct answer

Question ID: 156

Instead of managing Windows NT users individually, organize users into _____ so that rights and access privileges can be assigned to all members at once.

A.   Domains
B.   Sets
C.   Networks
D.   Clusters
E.   Groups

E is the correct answer

Question ID: 157

Select the default groups created during the Windows NT Workstation installation.

A.   Administrators
B.   Supervisors
C.   Power Users
D.   Everyone
E.   Management

A, C, and D are the correct answers

Question ID: 158

Which of the following default rights are assigned to Administrators, but not to Backup Operators in Windows NT?

A.   Access this computer from the network.
B.   Back up files and directories.
C.   Restore files and directories.
D.   Log on locally.

A is the correct answer

Question ID: 159

Greg is a member of the Power Users group on his Windows NT workstation. Select the action that Greg will NOT be able to perform.

    A. Access this system from a network.

    B. Change the system time.

    C. Manage auditing and the security log.

    D. Force a remote shutdown from another system.

    E. Copy files from one directory to another.

C is the correct answer

Question ID: 160

You are responsible for installing a spreadsheet application on your company's network. You want the employees to be able to access the application, but files they create will be saved in their home directory. What Windows NT permissions should you place on the directory where this application resides?

    A. Execute

    B. Write

    C. Modify

    D. Read

    E. Delete

A and D are the correct answers

Question ID: 161

You have a small network of 2 Windows NT Workstations. Both are using NTFS exclusively as their file system. You move a file from the first workstation to the second. Based on this information, which of the following statements are true?

    A. The file retains the same access permissions it had on the first workstation.

    B. The file inherits the access permissions found on the second workstation.

    C. The file becomes read only.

    D. The file loses all access permissions.

    E. None of the above

A is the correct answer

Question ID: 162

What is the maximum length for a username?

    A. 15 Characters

    B. 20 Characters

    C. 64 Characters

    D. 255 Characters

    E. There is no maximum length.

B is the correct answer

Question ID: 163

You would like Debra to manage the security logs for several workstations. Which group must you make Debra a member of in order to perform this task?

    A. Security Log Auditors

    B. Power Users

    C. Backup Operators

    D. Administrators

    E. Auditors

D is the correct answer

Question ID: 217

A customer calls with a problem with their Windows NT Workstation v4.0 computer. They are having trouble adding the username of 2WESTERN_sales-ASSOCIATES within User Manager. Which of the following statements explain why there is a problem?

    A. The underscore character is not allowed in a username.

    B. The dash character is not allowed in a username.

    C. The username exceeds the maximum length of 20 characters.

    D. All characters in a username must be in the same case.

    E. Digits are not allowed in a username.

C is the correct answer

Question ID: 218

By default, where are user logon scripts stored on a Windows NT computer?

    A. \WINNT\SYSTEM32\EXPORT\SCRIPTS

    B. \WINNT\SYSTEM32\IMPORT\SCRIPTS

    C. \WINNT\SYSTEM32\REPL\EXPORT\SCRIPTS

    D. \WINNT\SCRIPTS

    E. \WINNT\SYSTEM32\REPL\IMPORT\SCRIPTS

E is the correct answer

Question ID: 219

Who can view the Security Log in the Event Viewer?

    A. All members of the Power Users built-in group.

    B. All members of the Administrators built-in group.

    C. All members of the Replicator built-in group.

    D. All members of the Security Audit built-in group.

    E. All locally validated users.

B is the correct answer

Question ID: 276

Which utility (or utilities) allow(s) you to share directories to the network?

    A. Control Panel System

    B. Explorer

    C. Disk Administrator

    D. My Computer

    E. User Manager

B and D are the correct answers

Question ID: 277

Identify the statements that correctly describe file and directory auditing.

    A. Both successful and failed events may be audited.

    B. Audit information may be viewed by any user.

    C. Auditing is available on both NTFS and FAT partitions.

    D. An Administrator can clear the security log contents.

    E. Auditing applies equally to all users and groups.

A and D are the correct answers

Question ID: 278

When you copy a file from one directory to another under NTFS, what happens to its permissions?

    A. The permission settings are cleared.

    B. The permissions are set to match the destination directory.

    C. The permissions are unchanged.

    D. The user selects what will happen to permissions when the file is copied.

    E. There is no way to predict in advance.

B is the correct answer

Question ID: 279

When you move a file from one directory to another on the same volume under NTFS, what happens to its permissions?

    A. Permission settings are cleared.

    B. The permissions are set to match the destination directory.

    C. The permissions are unchanged.

    D. The user selects what will happen to permissions when the file is copied.

    E. There is no way to predict in advance.

C is the correct answer

Question ID: 280

A user belongs to the groups ACCT and FINANCE. The user is assigned Full Rights to a directory. The ACCT group is assigned Read and Execute. FINANCE is assigned No Access. What are the user's effective rights?

    A. Full Rights
    B. Read only
    C. Execute only
    D. Read and Execute
    E. No Access

E is the correct answer

Question ID: 317

Mary locked her workstation on the last day before her vacation and forgot to unlock and log off before leaving. You need to use her machine, but are afraid to turn it off and back on because it appears to be running something in the background. Who can unlock this workstation?

    A. Mary, when she returns from vacation
    B. Any power user
    C. Any administrator
    D. Any backup operator
    E. Any user

A and C are the correct answers

Question ID: 319

Which of the following fields are not copied when copying a user account definition?

    A. Username
    B. Group memberships
    C. Full Name
    D. Login script file
    E. Description

A and C are the correct answers

Question ID: 320

A user account name may contain up to _____ characters.

A. 8
B. 12
C. 16
D. 20
E. 32

D is the correct answer

Question ID: 321

When a user account is deleted, and then IMMEDIATELY re-created with the same account name:

A. All group memberships are retained.
B. All permissions and user rights remain the same.
C. File access permissions remain the same.
D. All group memberships, rights, and permissions are lost.
E. An error is generated.

D is the correct answer

Question ID: 322

User rights assignments are available to manage which of the following?

A. Network access to the workstation.
B. Local file access for file copy.
C. Local logon capabilities.
D. Ability to shut down the system.
E. Manual override of auditing.

A, C, and D are the correct answers

Question ID: 323

Which of the following rights are not assigned to Power Users?

- A. Change system time and date.
- B. Backup and restore all files.
- C. Log on locally.
- D. Take ownership of files or other objects.
- E. Shut down the system.

B and D are the correct answers

Question ID: 324

User rights are set through what utility?

- A. Server Manager
- B. User Manager
- C. System Administrator
- D. Disk Administrator
- E. Account Manager

B is the correct answer

Question ID: 325

What are the valid range of values for maximum password age?

- A. 1-30
- B. 1-60
- C. 1-90
- D. 1-365
- E. 1-999

E is the correct answer

Question ID: 326

The system is able to remember up to __ old passwords for any user.

   A. 2
   B. 8
   C. 12
   D. 24
   E. 32

D is the correct answer

Question ID: 327

System-wide password management settings are known as:

   A. Restrictions.
   B. Permissions.
   C. Rights.
   D. Policies.
   E. There is no special term.

D is the correct answer

Question ID: 328

Which of the following are not valid characters for usernames?

   A. Lowercase letters
   B. Uppercase letters
   C. !
   D. \
   E. ?

D and E are the correct answers

Question ID: 329

When modifying multiple users, you cannot change:

A. Username.
B. Full Name.
C. Password.
D. Profile name.
E. Home directory.

A, B, and C are the correct answers

Question ID: 330

Which of the following settings will help users to select more secure passwords?

A. Set a minimum password length
B. Set a maximum password length
C. Enable password uniqueness
D. Enable account lockout
E. Set an account expiration date

A and C are the correct answers

Question ID: 341

Stoltz & Co., a small medical research company, is using Windows NT Workstation on network workstations. Stanley Miller needs to be able to manage auditing and the security log on any workstation. He is also authorized to override locked workstations. He should be a member of what group on all workstations?

A. Power Users
B. Backup Operators
C. Users
D. Administrators
E. Guests

D is the correct answer

Question ID: 342

Mike does not require the ability to manage auditing and the security log. His duties in the company require him to be able to change system time, assign user rights, and share and stop sharing of directories and printers. He should be a member of what Windows NT Workstation group?

A. Replicators
B. Users
C. Administrators
D. Backup Operators
E. Power Users

E is the correct answer

Question ID: 348

Your company, Crystal Works Inc., is concerned with monitoring network security. Crystal wants to maintain a close, careful watch on the security log. Only members of what group may access the security log?

A. Adminstrators only
B. Administrators and Backup Operators
C. Administrators and Power Users
D. Administrators, Power Users, and Users

A is the correct answer

Macintosh

MACINTOSH CONFIGURATION

For review of this topic, refer to Chapter 1.

Question ID: 12

The icon for Disk First Aid is:

    A.   A repairman with a red cross on his shirt.
    B.   A doctor.
    C.   A hammer, shovel, and screwdriver.
    D.   An ambulance.

D is the correct answer

Question ID: 13

Which of the following will Disk First Aid do? (Choose all that apply.)

    A.   Initialize or format a hard drive.
    B.   Diagnose floppy diskettes problems.
    C.   Fix hard drive problems.
    D.   Fix floppy drive problems.

B, C, and D are the correct answers

Question ID: 14

The Apple HD SC Program is used to:

    A.   Initialize hard disks.
    B.   Repair floppy diskettes.
    C.   Create icons for documents.
    D.   Reinstall the Finder program.

A is the correct answer

Question ID: 39

The Chooser is used to: (Choose all that apply.)

A. Select a new printer.
B. Select a network.
C. Turn AppleTalk off and on.
D. Toggle between applications.

A, B, and C are the correct answers

Question ID: 78

Which are major steps in setting up a Macintosh? (Choose all that apply.)

A. Turning on the system.
B. Connecting the monitor, keyboard, and power cord.
C. Connecting the Microprocessor.
D. Removing all components from their boxes.

A, B, and D are the correct answers

Question ID: 79

Which of the following devices are connected to a Macintosh using the ADB?

A. Mouse
B. Printer
C. Keyboard
D. External modem

A and C are the correct answers

Question ID: 80

Some Macintosh computers can be started by:

A. Pressing the Power key on the keyboard.
B. Double-clicking the mouse.
C. Holding the <Apple> key and then pressing the letter "s".
D. Holding the <Shift> key while double-clicking the mouse.

A is the correct answer

Question ID: 81

What step must be completed before installing a video adapter in a Macintosh? (Choose all that apply.)

- A. Turn the monitor on.
- B. Ground yourself against electrostatic discharge.
- C. Install memory chips.
- D. Upgrade to system 7.5.

B is the correct answer

Question ID: 82

What program is run to install or upgrade the Macintosh Operating System?

- A. Setup
- B. Upgrader
- C. Installer
- D. Apple System Software

C is the correct answer

Question ID: 86

What must be selected after selecting a printer in Chooser? (Choose all that apply.)

- A. The port or network name of the printer.
- B. The time zone.
- C. The speed of the printer.
- D. How many colors it will print.

A is the correct answer

Question ID: 89

To correct a damaged System folder, you should: (Choose all that apply.)

    A. Use the Disk Tools diskette to run the "Correct System Folder" utility.
    B. Perform a Clean Installation of the Mac OS.
    C. Use Apple HD SC setup to correct the problems in the System folder.
    D. Reinitialize the hard drive and reinstall the Mac OS.
    E. Drag the System folder to the Trash Can.

B is the correct answer

Question ID: 96

Initializing diskettes:

    A. Is a two-step process.
    B. Takes five to ten minutes for each side.
    C. Cannot be done if the Macintosh is connected to a file server.
    D. Can only be done on the internal disk drive.

A is the correct answer

Question ID: 97

Which disk drive can prepare diskettes that can also be used on a DOS system?

    A. 400 KB
    B. 800 KB
    C. SuperDrive
    D. SmartDrive

C is the correct answer

Question ID: 98

When initializing a diskette, you will be asked to type in a name for a diskette, unless:

    A.   The fast initialize option is picked.

    B.   The disk has been formatted on a DOS system.

    C.   The disk has been previously named.

    D.   The disk is going to be used as a bootable disk.

C is the correct answer

Question ID: 100

SCSI stands for:

    A.   Standard Computer System Interface.

    B.   Small Communication System Interface.

    C.   Small Computer System Interface.

    D.   Synchronized Computer System Interface.

C is the correct answer

Question ID: 101

Which of the following devices can be connected to the Apple Desktop Bus?

    A.   Speakers

    B.   Joystick

    C.   Keyboard

    D.   Mouse

B, C, and D are the correct answers

Question ID: 110

Which statements about SuperDrive diskette drives are true? (Choose all that apply.)

    A. SuperDrive supports the use of 400 KB, 800 KB, or 1.4 MB diskettes.

    B. SuperDrive can format a diskette in DOS format.

    C. SuperDrive drives are not supported in PowerPC models.

    D. SuperDrive can read high-density diskettes formatted by the DOS operating system.

A, B, and D are the correct answers

Question ID: 125

You have just installed a new SCSI hard disk drive in a Macintosh system. It is the only hard disk drive installed in the computer and will act as the system's startup disk. The documentation accompanying the new drive is very generic and does not contain any specific information on Macintosh installation. In addition, no Macintosh disk utilities or drivers were provided. Which tasks must you perform to prepare the new hard disk drive for a Mac OS 8 installation?

    A. Start the Macintosh by booting from the Mac OS CD, double-click on the Disk First Aid icon in the Utilities folder, select the SCSI disk drive and click on the Initialize button.

    B. Start the Macintosh by booting from the Mac OS CD, double-click on the Disk Prep icon in the Utilities folder, select the SCSI disk drive and click on the Initialize button.

    C. Start the Macintosh by booting from the Mac OS CD, double-click on the Drive Setup icon in the Utilities folder, select the SCSI disk drive and click on the Initialize button.

    D. Start the Macintosh by booting from the Mac OS CD, double-click on the Disk Init icon in the Utilities folder, select the SCSI disk drive and click on the Initialize button.

C is the correct answer

Question ID: 126

A user has called the Help Desk complaining that they can no longer start their Macintosh workstation. After asking several questions you discover that the user was in the process of upgrading the system to Mac OS 8 when the trouble began. You are unsure of whether the user's Macintosh computer meets the minimum hardware requirements for Mac OS 8. Which of the following questions should you ask the user to determine whether Mac OS 8 can successfully be installed on their computer?

A. Does the computer have a minimum of 8 MB of physical RAM?
B. Does the computer have a minimum of 12 MB of physical RAM?
C. Does the hard disk drive have at least 45 MB of free space available?
D. Does the hard disk drive have at least 95 MB of free space available?

B and D are the correct answers

MACINTOSH OPERATING SYSTEM

For review of this topic, refer to Chapter 2.

Question ID: 35

The purpose of the Finder is to:

A. Find lost files, much like the "Find" function in Windows 95.
B. Manage the desktop and act as the operating system on Macintosh computers.
C. Switch between open applications.
D. Find system information such as how much RAM is free.

B is the correct answer

Question ID: 36

The Trash Can icon may be used to:

A. Quit applications.
B. Permanently delete files and eject diskettes.
C. Reformat disks.
D. Recover files which have been deleted.
E. Create and delete temporary files.

B is the correct answer

Question ID: 37

Which of the following statements about the Scrapbook is true? (Choose all that apply.)

A. Contents are replaced as soon as another item is copied.
B. Provides a RAM address in which to store several items.
C. Is a ROM function and can not be disabled.
D. Is a desk accessory found under the Apple menu.

D is the correct answer

Question ID: 38

In which pull-down menu is the Chooser located?

A. Applications Menu
B. Control Panels
C. Edit Menu
D. Apple Menu

D is the correct answer

Question ID: 40

Where is the Erase Disk command found?

A. The Desktop
B. The Special Menu
C. The File Menu
D. The Chooser

B is the correct answer

Question ID: 41

Pressing the keys <Apple><E> causes the system to:

A. Erase the startup diskette.
B. Edit the selected document.
C. Eject a diskette.
D. Print an envelope.
E. Rebuild the Desktop.

C is the correct answer

Question ID: 42

To remove a diskette icon from the desktop: (Choose all that apply.)

    A. Select Eject Disk from the Special Menu.
    B. Drag the diskette icon to the System Folder.
    C. Drag the diskette icon to the Trash.
    D. Select Cut from the Edit Menu.

A and C are the correct answers

Question ID: 43

A flashing question mark (?) means:

    A. The system cannot find the System and Finder files.
    B. The system cannot find a bootable disk.
    C. The system cannot read the disk that was inserted.
    D. The system cannot find the boot record in the file allocation table.

B is the correct answer

Question ID: 44

Extensions or inits are loaded when:

    A. The "Happy Mac" screen is displayed.
    B. The system is restarted.
    C. The "Welcome to Macintosh" screen is displayed.
    D. The desktop appears.

C is the correct answer

Question ID: 45

A flashing "X" means the system cannot:

    A. Find either the System or Finder files.
    B. Find a disk.
    C. Read a disk that was inserted.
    D. Find the boot record in the file allocation table.

A is the correct answer

Question ID: 46

The System and Finder files are stored in the:

- A. Control Panel Folder.
- B. Startup Folder.
- C. Applications Folder.
- D. System Folder.

D is the correct answer

Question ID: 47

When more than one System Folder exists on a startup disk, the Macintosh will: (Choose all that apply.)

- A. Display a System Bomb dialog box.
- B. Load the system with the highest revision number.
- C. Choose one to load.
- D. Delete the System Folder with the earliest date.

C is the correct answer

Question ID: 48

Almost all Toolbox Routines are stored:

- A. In ROM.
- B. In the System Folder.
- C. In a folder labeled Toolbox.
- D. In Control Panel.

A is the correct answer

Question ID: 49

The purpose of the Finder is to _____ the desktop.

A. Color
B. Manage
C. Maximize
D. Arrange

B is the correct answer

Question ID: 50

When dragged to the System Folder, extensions and fonts are automatically placed in their respective folders:

A. In System 6.
B. In all System versions.
C. Only in System 7 or higher.
D. They cannot be automatically placed.

C is the correct answer

Question ID: 51

In System 7, the Control Panel is accessed from the: (Choose all that apply.)

A. Applications Menu.
B. Apple Menu.
C. File Menu.
D. System Folder.

B and D are the correct answers

Question ID: 52

Which of the following is a Control Panel Device? (Choose all that apply.)

A. Brightness
B. Keycaps
C. General Controls
D. Cache switch

A, C, and D are the correct answers

Question ID: 53

What are the lower-level programs from which applications draw resources? (Choose all that apply.)

A. User Interface Toolbox
B. Operating System
C. Desktop
D. Apple Desktop Bus System

A and B are the correct answers

Question ID: 54

The Desktop is used to manage: (Choose all that apply.)

A. Files only.
B. Disks only.
C. The menu bar.
D. Files and disks.

D is the correct answer

Question ID: 55

The Menu Bar is located at the _____ of the desktop.

A. Top
B. Bottom
C. Left
D. Right

A is the correct answer

Question ID: 56

One of the major components of the Desktop is the:

A. Organizer.
B. Control Panel.
C. Disk Tools icon.
D. Chooser.
E. Trash Can.

E is the correct answer

Question ID: 57

The Application Menu appears:

A. In System 6 only.
B. In System 7 only.
C. Only if activated in the Control Panel.
D. None of the above

B is the correct answer

Question ID: 58

The Apple Menu is visible:

    A.   All the time.

    B.   When word processing programs are the active window.

    C.   During the installation of the Macintosh Operating System.

    D.   If the Apple Menu extension is dragged to the System folder.

A is the correct answer

Question ID: 59

The top option under the Apple Menu is:

    A.   System Information...

    B.   Desk Accessories

    C.   About This...

    D.   Chooser

C is the correct answer

Question ID: 60

The Trash Can may be used to: (Choose all that apply.)

    A.   Remove unwanted documents or files.

    B.   Remove unwanted folders.

    C.   Eject diskettes.

    D.   Reformat disks.

    E.   Delete temporary files.

A, B, and C are the correct answers

Question ID: 61

Horizontal lines in the title bar of a window indicates:

    A. The window is the active window.

    B. The window is a disk.

    C. The window is a network resource.

    D. The window has a virus.

A is the correct answer

Question ID: 62

To close a window, click on the box located:

    A. At the top of the vertical scroll bar.

    B. In the upper right corner of the window.

    C. In the upper left corner of the window.

    D. At the left of the horizontal scroll bar.

C is the correct answer

Question ID: 63

The Installer program is used to:

    A. Install the Macintosh Operating System.

    B. Install vendor software, such as word processors.

    C. Provide a map of the IRQs used on the system.

    D. Install and initialize a hard drive.

    E. Update the Macintosh Operating System.

A and E are the correct answers

Question ID: 64

The "background area" is better known as:

    A.   The wallpaper.
    B.   The grey area.
    C.   The Desktop.
    D.   The system heap.
    E.   The application space.

C is the correct answer

Question ID: 65

The Application Menu allows you to do which of the following?

    A.   Quickly see a list of application programs that are loaded on the Macintosh.
    B.   Quickly launch any application programs that are loaded on the Macintosh.
    C.   Set the priority for multitasking operations among open applications.
    D.   Quickly switch between applications that are open.

D is the correct answer

Question ID: 67

On a Macintosh, at what point in the startup process are extensions loaded?

    A.   When the desktop appears.
    B.   After the first tone is heard.
    C.   They are dynamically loaded as needed.
    D.   When the "Welcome to Macintosh" screen appears.

D is the correct answer

Question ID: 68

In System 7, where is the Eject Disk command found?

    A. The File Menu.

    B. The Apple Menu.

    C. The Applications Menu.

    D. The Special Menu.

D is the correct answer

Question ID: 69

On a Macintosh using System 6, where would you look to see a list of all currently active applications?

    A. The File Menu.

    B. The Applications Menu.

    C. The Multi-Finder Menu.

    D. The Apple Menu.

D is the correct answer

Question ID: 70

Which of the following statements about common inits and extensions are true? (Choose all that apply.)

    A. The Graphics Accelerator provides video acceleration for PCI video cards.

    B. The Network extension allows you to set Personal File Sharing from the Finder.

    C. The MacinTalk extension allows your Macintosh to respond to voice commands.

    D. PrintMonitor allows you to control the printing process on a Mac.

    E. QuickTime provides built-in multimedia support for your Mac.

A, B, D, and E are the correct answers

Question ID: 71

You can turn off extensions or inits that you do not wish to load using the:

    A.   Installer
    B.   Disk Tools
    C.   Extensions Manager
    D.   Apple HD SC Setup
    E.   Application Menu

C is the correct answer

Question ID: 72

Which of the following statements about common inits and extensions are false? (Choose all that apply.)

    A.   The Shortcuts extension manages shortcuts and aliases within the Mac OS.
    B.   The EM extension works with the Extensions Manager control panel, specifying which extensions are turned on at system startup.
    C.   The Finder Scripting extension allows you to use AppleScript to automate tasks in the Finder.
    D.   The Finder Help extension provides Balloon Help support for the Finder.

A is the correct answer

Question ID: 74

Which of the following statements about common commands used in Macintosh applications are true? (Choose all that apply.)

    A.   <Command><X> cuts a selected item to the clipboard.
    B.   <Command><Option><Escape> will force an application to quit.
    C.   <Command><V> pastes the clipboard contents into the selection.
    D.   <Command><W> closes the active window.

A, B, C, and D are the correct answers

Question ID: 108

A startup disk must:

A.   Contain a startup folder.
B.   Contain System and Finder files.
C.   Be an internal disk drive.
D.   Be a hard disk drive.

B is the correct answer

Question ID: 109

What is the minimum amount of RAM required to run System 7?

A.   1 MB
B.   2 MB
C.   4 MB
D.   8 MB

B is the correct answer

Question ID: 127

A Macintosh Startup disk must contain which of the following files?

A.   Chooser
B.   System
C.   Finder
D.   Extensions Manager

B and C are the correct answers

Question ID: 130

You have been asked to assist a customer that is having several problems with their Macintosh system. They can no longer access shared folders in the Chooser, their CD-ROM drive is not working, and most of the Control Panels are missing. After inquiring about the events that led to the current condition, the user supplies you with the following information: "The system was functioning normally until I copied several folders from a shared network disk volume. Even after the copy process completed, the computer worked great until I restarted it." Which of the following scenarios most likely describes the source of the failure?

    A. The Chooser application is corrupted.
    B. There is a problem with the system's Startup disk.
    C. The user copied a second System Foler onto their Startup Disk.
    D. The Control Panels folder is damaged.

C is the correct answer

Question ID: 131

Which of the following System software components provides the interface to Macintosh system hardware?

    A. User Interface Toolbox
    B. Menu Manager
    C. Finder
    D. Mac OS

D is the correct answer

Question ID: 132

Almost all of the Macintosh low-level Toolbox and Operating System routines are stored _____.

    A. In the System file.
    B. In Read Only Memory (ROM).
    C. In the System Folder.
    D. On the Startup disk.

B is the correct answer

Question ID: 133

The Macintosh System Folder contains which of the following items?

A. System file
B. Finder
C. Control Panels
D. Extensions
E. Desktop file

A, B, C, and D are the correct answers

Question ID: 134

Which two of the following are components of the Macintosh Desktop?

A. Startup disk
B. Menu bar
C. Background area
D. Chooser utility

B and D are the correct answers

Question ID: 135

The Chooser is a Desk Accessory _____.

A. Lets users enable or diable system Control Panels and Extensions.
B. Lets users customize the appearance of the Desktop and Apple menu.
C. Lets users select devices connected directly to local printer or modem ports, or devices on an AppleTalk network.
D. Lets users manage files and folders on the Desktop and shared network folders located on other Macintosh systems.

C is the correct answer

Question ID: 137

What must you do to bypass a Macintosh Startup disk and boot from a Mac OS system CD-ROM?

A.   Start or restart the computer while holding down <Command><Option> <Shift><Delete>.

B.   Start or restart the computer while holding down <Command><Option> <Shift><Delete>.

C.   Start or restart the computer while holding down <Command><Shift> <Delete>.

D.   Start or restart the computer while holding down <Command><Option> <Delete>.

A is the correct answer

Question ID: 149

Which of the following key combination will cause a Macintosh system to reboot?

A.   <Control><Option><Shift><Delete>

B.   <Control><Command><Power>

C.   <Command><Control><Delete>

D.   <Command><Shift><Delete>

B is the correct answer

MACINTOSH NETWORKING

For review of this topic, refer to Chapter 3.

Question ID: 21

When logging on to a server, Guest is dimmed because:

A. There is not a user named Guest.

B. The monitor could be malfunctioning.

C. You must press <Apple> key <G> to highlight Guest.

D. Guest does not have access to that file server.

D is the correct answer

Question ID: 24

Which of the following statements about LocalTalk cables is most correct?

A. LocalTalk cables are available only from Apple.

B. LocalTalk cables can be used to connect a modem to the Macintosh.

C. LocalTalk cables are available from either Apple or third-party vendors.

D. LocalTalk cables are custom made from telephone wire.

C is the correct answer

Question ID: 25

Installing an Ethernet or Token Ring adapter into a Macintosh _____:

A. Is not possible.

B. Is unneccesary, since AppleTalk is already installed.

C. Gives a faster data transfer rate than AppleTalk.

D. Is too costly to be practical, because hardware upgrades are required.

C is the correct answer

Question ID: 26

For what purpose was LocalTalk primarily designed?

    A.   Connecting Macintosh systems to a Macintosh file server.

    B.   Connecting Macintosh systems in a peer-to-peer configuration.

    C.   Connecting Macintosh systems to networked SCSI devices.

    D.   Connecting a Macintosh workgroup to shared printers.

D is the correct answer

Question ID: 27

What type of cable cannot be installed on a LocalTalk protocol network?

    A.   Shielded twisted-pair (STP) cable

    B.   Coaxial cable

    C.   Telephone wire

    D.   Any of the above will work.

B is the correct answer

Question ID: 28

LocalTalk networks are:

    A.   Faster than either EtherTalk or TokenTalk networks, if only Macs are connected.

    B.   Slower than TokenTalk networks, but faster than EtherTalk networks.

    C.   Slower than either EtherTalk or TokenTalk networks.

    D.   The same speed as any other network involving Macintoshes, since the AppleTalk phase 2 protocol was introduced.

C is the correct answer

Question ID: 30

AppleTalk is: (Choose all that apply.)

    A. Activated using the Chooser.

    B. Inactive when a scanner is attached.

    C. Only used if an Ethernet or Token Ring adapter is installed.

    D. Can be used with an ArcNet adapter.

A is the correct answer

Question ID: 31

To name your Macintosh for a network: (Choose all that apply.)

    A. Select Name the Mac from the Special Menu.

    B. Select Sharing Setup from Control Panel.

    C. Select New User from the File Menu.

    D. A Network administrator must be contacted.

B is the correct answer

Question ID: 32

What are the user types in a file server? (Choose all that apply.)

    A. Owners

    B. Guests

    C. Programmers

    D. Registered users

    E. Supervisors

A, B, and D are the correct answers

Question ID: 34

On a file server, you become the owner of a folder: (Choose all that apply.)

A. If the owner transfers ownership to you.
B. When you create it.
C. When you open it.
D. When you access it.

A and B are the correct answers

Question ID: 138

Which of the following network communication protocols are supported by Mac OS 8?

A. AppleTalk
B. NetBEUI
C. TCP/IP
D. IPX

A, C, and D are the correct answers

Question ID: 140

TokenTalk networks can transmit data at _____.

A. 10 megabits per second.
B. 100 megabits per second.
C. 16 megabits per second.
D. 230.4 kilobits per second.

C is the correct answer

Question ID: 141

The Macintosh networking architecture introduced in System 7.5 is called:

A. Classic Macintosh networking.
B. MacTCP.
C. Open Protocols.
D. Open Transport.

D is the correct answer

Question ID: 142

Which of the following parameters can be specified using the AppleTalk Control Panel?

    A. Subnet mask
    B. Connection port
    C. Workstation IP address
    D. AppleTalk zone

B and D are the correct answers

Question ID: 143

A user phones the Help desk complaining that they cannot print to any network printers. You ask them to verify that the AppleTalk Control Panel and AppleShare Extension are activated by using the Extensions Manager utility. The user confirms that both items are checked and that the AppleTalk Control Panel is available and properly configured. How should you instruct the user to see if AppleTalk is active?

    A. Open the Network Control Panel and see if the AppleTalk box is checked.
    B. Open the AppleTalk Control Panel and see if the Networking box is checked.
    C. Open the Chooser and see if AppleTalk is active.
    D. Open the Finder and see if AppleTalk is active.

C is the correct answer

Question ID: 144

Which of the following protocols may be used to automate the assignment of Macintosh IP addresses?

    A. BootP
    B. WINS
    C. DHCP
    D. RARP

A, C, and D are the correct answers

Question ID: 145

Which protocol is used by Macintosh system for dial-up connections to the Internet?

A. RAS

B. Dial-up IP

C. PPP

D. DHCP

C is the correct answer

Question ID: 150

LocalTalk networks can be constructed using which of the following cable types?

A. RG-58 coaxial cable

B. Shielded Twisted-Pair (STP) cable

C. IBM Type 1 cable

D. Standard phone cable

B and D are the correct answers

DIAGNOSIS AND REPAIR

For review of this topic, refer to Chapter 4.

Question ID: 18

The "sad Macintosh" face appearing immediately at power up signifies a
_____.

    A. Software Problem.

    B. Hardware Problem.

    C. User operation error.

    D. All of the above

    E. None of the above

B is the correct answer

Question ID: 19

You have selected the AppleShare icon in Chooser but do not see the file server you want. What is the next step you should take?

    A. Reload the Operating System making sure that all AppleShare extensions are loaded.

    B. Check the SCSI connection to see if the AppleShare cable has worked loose.

    C. Pick the zone that contains the file server you want.

    D. Check the System Folder to be sure that all AppleShare extensions are in the Networks Folder.

C is the correct answer

Question ID: 76

Which of the following programs are provided with the Macintosh Operating System to help correct problems with diskettes or hard drives?

    A. Disk First Aid

    B. Installer

    C. HD SC Setup

    D. Font/DA Mover

A is the correct answer

Question ID: 77

Which of the following programs are provided with the Macintosh Operating System to help set up hard drives?

A. Disk First Aid
B. Installer
C. HD SC Setup
D. Font/DA Mover

C is the correct answer

Question ID: 111

You press the Power button on the keyboard. The power light does not come on, the Macintosh screen is black, the startup tone is not heard and the Happy Mac icon does not appear. What is the first question to ask the customer?

A. Is the system under warranty?
B. Is the monitor cable connected to the Macintosh?
C. Can the startup disk be opened?
D. Is the power cord connected to the Macintosh and an outlet?

D is the correct answer

Question ID: 113

A customer calls and explains the Macintosh operation system loaded okay, but when the mouse is moved, the pointer does not move. Your first question should be:

A. Is the keyboard connected to the ADB port of the Macintosh?
B. Was the mouse option chosen when the operating system was installed?
C. Is the printer turned on and ready?
D. What kind of monitor is connected to the Macintosh?

A is the correct answer

Question ID: 114

The Sad Mac icon is displayed:

    A. When the system detects a virus.

    B. When the mouse is double-clicked too fast.

    C. When the printer can not be found.

    D. When the Mac detects an error with a disk drive, memory, or logic board.

D is the correct answer

Question ID: 115

How many times will the Mac sound a tone to indicate it has completed the POST test?

    A. 1

    B. 2

    C. 3

    D. 4

A is the correct answer

Question ID: 116

How many tones will be heard if the Mac detects a problem with memory?

    A. 4

    B. 6

    C. 8

    D. 10

C is the correct answer

Question ID: 118

What is the result of pressing <Option><Command><R><P> simultaneously? (Choose all that apply.)

- A. Any software patches to ROM are cleared.
- B. Parameter RAM settings are cleared.
- C. A dialog box displays the ROM BIOS version.
- D. A program that is hung is restarted.

B is the correct answer

Question ID: 119

What key combination is pressed while a Macintosh is restarting to rebuild the desktop?

- A. <Control><Option>
- B. <Option> at Startup
- C. <Control><Command>
- D. <Shift><Control><Option>

B is the correct answer

Question ID: 120

After a configuration change, a user cannot print. What should you have the user check to assist in troubleshooting the problem?

- A. Make sure that the proper printer is selected in the Control Panel.
- B. Have the user restart the Macintosh with Extensions disabled.
- C. Perform a clean installation of the Mac OS.
- D. Make sure that the proper printer is selected in the Chooser.

D is the correct answer

Question ID: 121

After reconfiguring a Macintosh system, a user finds that they cannot access resources on the network. What can you have the user do to troubleshoot this problem?

    A.   Make sure that AppleTalk is active in the Chooser.
    B.   Perform a clean installation of the Mac OS.
    C.   Zap the PRAM by pressing <Command><Option><R><P> simultaneously.
    D.   Have the user restart the Macintosh with Extensions disabled.
    E.   Rebuild the Desktop by pressing <Option> while restarting the Macintosh.

A is the correct answer

Question ID: 122

When using System 7.5 or later, pressing and holding the <Spacebar> during system startup:

    A.   Zaps the PRAM.
    B.   Rebuilds the Desktop.
    C.   Activates AppleShare.
    D.   Ejects any floppy diskettes.
    E.   Opens the Extensions Manager.

E is the correct answer

Question ID: 123

If a Macintosh freezes while idle, a likely cause could be:

    A.   A corrupt System folder.
    B.   The Desktop needs rebuilt.
    C.   A Screen Saver could be freezing the system.
    D.   The processor is failing.

C is the correct answer

Question ID: 128

A user calls the Help desk complaining that their Macintosh workstation would not start properly this morning. The user cycled the computer's power switch several times and heard the normal Macintosh startup "chimes" sound. Each startup attempt displayed a flashing "X" on the monitor. What is the most likely source of this system's failure?

    A.   There is a problem with one of the memory modules installed on the system board.

    B.   The Macintosh power supply is failing.

    C.   The Startup disk cannot be located.

    D.   The Macintosh cannot find the System Folder.

D is the correct answer

Question ID: 129

Your Macintosh is used as a digital video workstation and boots from an external RAID disk array. You have just switched on the power and after hearing the normal "chimes" startup sound you see a flashing "?" displayed on the monitor. Why is the flashing "?" displayed?

    A.   The Macintosh system board has failed.

    B.   The RAID disk array is not powered on or has failed.

    C.   There is a problem with one of the memory modules installed on the system board.

    D.   An Extensions conflict is preventing the system from starting up properly.

B is the correct answer

Question ID: 136

Each time your Macintosh computer is started, it locks up. Everything appears to be working properly. The startup "chimes" are heard and the Welcome to Macintosh screen is displayed. What should you do to locate the source of the problem?

A. Restart the Macintosh while holding down the the <Option> key, until the Welcome to Macintosh screen appears. Next, use the Extensions Manager to disable all unneeded Control Panels and Extensions

B. Restart the Macintosh while holding down the the <Shift> key until the Welcome to Macintosh screen appears. Next, use the Extensions Manager to disable all unneeded Control Panels and Extensions.

C. Restart the Macintosh while holding down <Command><Option> until the Welcome to Macintosh screen appears. Next, use the Extensions Manager to disable all unneeded Control Panels and Extensions.

D. Restart the Macintosh while holding down <Control><Option> until the Welcome to Macintosh screen appears. Next, use the Extensions Manager to disable all unneeded Control Panels and Extensions.

B is the correct answer

Question ID: 146

What does the Sad Mac graphic indicate during the Macintosh system startup procedure?

A. The Startup disk cannot be located.
B. There is a hardware problem with the diskette drive, memory, or logic board.
C. There is a problem with the power supply.
D. The Startup disk is damaged.

B is the correct answer

Question ID: 147

Which of the following may cause the pointer to not move when the mouse is moved?

A. The mouse is defective.
B. The serial port is defective.
C. The ADB port is defective.
D. The mouse connection may have failed.

A, C, and D are the correct answers

Question ID: 148

What is the last resort for removing a floppy diskette that will not eject from a Macintosh diskette drive?

A. Shut down the Macintosh.
B. Hold down the mouse button while powering the system on.
C. Select Eject Diskette from th Finder File menu.
D. Insert the end of a paper clip into the small hole located to the right of the diskette drive and push firmly.

D is the correct answer